SANDY ROW

BORN AND BRED

SANDY ROW

BORN AND BRED

By Victor Gordon Skelly Freeman

Dedicated to the Sandy Row Community, past, present and future.

That which hath been is now; and that which is to be hath already been; and God requireth that which is past.

– Ecclesiastes 3:15.

Foreword

I first met Gordon Freeman when he taught a Bible class in Primitive Street Methodist Church, but it was when I started work at the Ulster Museum in 1969 that I really got to know Gordon. He was already working there as a supervisor and was later promoted to Chief Warder. As we both had deep family roots with Sandy Row, our conversations during break times often turned to the events that were going on in the Row during what has become known as the Troubles. Gordon felt that the Sandy Row he knew was being lost and in response put many of his thoughts into his degree work at Queen's University Belfast, where he was a mature student. In addition, he started to write about his family and Sandy Row, and it was his wish that his writings would become a book. Sadly Gordon died on 5th November 1984. Some time before his death he gave me the manuscript, which was in his own handwriting. I arranged to have it typed. The typist sometimes had to guess some words, however, having the words typed was a great help. Every effort has been made not to change wording but in a few places it was found necessary. I have added some additional information which you will see written in italics.

Billy Dickson BEM
Chair: Blackstaff Residents' Association
Former Alderman & Deputy Lord Mayor of Belfast

Introduction

Conventional writings on childhood memories usually begin with our first recorded reaching out, as an inexperienced but nevertheless unique and independent ego. An ego which has already formed a known pattern of events and remembering of its own, thus 'All I could ever be all men ignored in me, thus was I worth to God, whose wheel the pitcher shaped.' What I am about to relate in the following chapters deviates from the norm and in so doing comes under the heading of 'Sandy Row Born and Bred'. It is not entirely dependent on any conscious remembering on my part, but belongs to that important contributing factor in our lives which I have described as breeding. That something which quite often in no small measure had affected our attitudes and character long before we ever materialized as a twinkle in our parents' eyes and must necessarily belong to the moral standards and stances of others around us, namely our parents. Consequently, it is a rather shadowy world full of furtive figures and strange smells and which, apart from those occasional moments of revealed insight (like some forms of conversion), we must accept as coming to us at best second-hand. Therefore it behoves us to examine with specific interest the Principal Egos which, unsought by us, have to no small degree overshadowed our own and which, whether we are prepared to acknowledge it or not, have already prejudiced our own feelings towards our surroundings and in no small measure shaped our own behaviour patterns. Motivated with these considerations in mind I have attempted in my opening chapter to lay bare the idiosyncrasies and social attitudes surrounding my early upbringing and in so doing beg the reader's indulgence.

Victor Gordon Skelly Freeman

Chapter 1
12 Gaffikin Street

When the midwife, known by name as Aggie Rea and by vocation as the local stork in the district, called in our humble home at 12 Gaffikin Street, it was to deliver Big Lil, as she was affectionately known by my father, of a bouncing baby boy. From that moment I was endowed with a uniqueness which, for obvious reasons, is now given only to a few of her sons. I was Sandy Row born. No hospital for me, indeed no welfare state, Oyster Milk or Cow & Gate, but Arrowroot biscuits crushed in warm milk and all the love that a Zechariah and Elizabeth could give to a long-awaited arrival.

My parents, David and Elizabeth had been married for years, with no offspring as a sign of the consummation of their marriage. In their bitter disappointment, they had fostered a child who, to their pain and anguish, was later taken from them, and though no comets appeared in the sky, the year 1934 brought with it no promised panacea for the world's problems. Sinister forces were on the move in Germany as Nazism cast its dark and frightening shadow across the continent of Europe. A few years later and Spain was involved in a bloody and brutal civil war, and of course we always had the potential and all the ingredients for sectarian violence in Belfast (the following year, 1935, witnessed the worst street riots ever recorded). Unemployment, the arch-enemy of civilized society, and no stranger to the people of Belfast and this Island, stretched the minds of the ablest of the world's politicians.

Nevertheless, my advent, when it came, was not allowed to go by unnoticed and without a sense of the importance of the occasion. Much to my later dismay, confusion and at times a deep feeling of embarrassment, I was to be known henceforth to the world by the prodigious title of Master Victor Gordon Skelly Freeman and baptized at no less an edifice than St. Anne's Cathedral.

Incorporated into my name was that of a favourite brother-in-law of my father's, Gordon S. Kelly: a sort of legendary and, by all accounts, brash and impulsive figure who many years previous to my birth had emigrated to Windsor, Ontario in Canada, and whose exploits were often discussed with a great deal of merriment and vigour around our fireside of an evening. My uncle, apparently, was regarded as a kindly-disposed sort of person with a seemingly different pugilistic type of temperament and an outlook secular as opposed to sacred, who was not above playing with my grandmother's cat while the visiting clergyman conducted family prayers in the small kitchen of their home.

Regarding the imposing location of my baptism, I was later to learn that the reason for my baptism at such a place was not connected to any special feeling of importance for my arrival in the world, but rather because my father was able to take the fullest advantage out of which the popularity of such a place afforded him. It was brought about, as my mother later explained, because no great pressure was put upon the male parent to attend, and so my father, who regarded births, deaths and marriages with the amount of reserve and suspicion which the buying of a new suit on such occasions called for, predictably absented himself. So conditioned was he that he only appeared at my brother's wedding on the understanding that he was only allowed to turn out for such a rare family event clad in a new suit from the local second-hand shop. In an age dominated by moneylenders and tick men, a new suit represented an unnecessary outlay of hard-earned cash (the result of long hours of sweat and toil as Ward Master in the Workhouse) and cost more than his meagre salary afforded him. It sometimes represented the difference between keeping one's head above water and falling into the hands of unscrupulous men. So there I was, one among sixty odd infants all clamouring for recognition in a time-honoured way. Among such maternal confusion and excitement, my father's absence didn't even raise a ripple in the baptismal stream. Probably conscious, no doubt, that his cloth cap and shiny black suit, with boots to match, would only look out of place in such an impressive assembly.

His utter selflessness has always been an inspiration to me and though, as he called them 'the good old bad days' have long ceased to cast their shadows over our lives, and he is no more, down the memories of the years I can still hear him as he arrived home from the Workhouse, tired and weary, as we gathered around our well-scrubbed table covered by the local newspaper, 'Lil, has everyone got enough?' refusing to begin his simple meal until my mother assured him that we had all eaten. The most important lessons life has taught me came from my early childhood, handed down to me by my father's example.

A devout Orangeman all his life, my father could proudly boast to being the youngest lecturer in the Orange Order. He was a member of the Loyal Orange Lodge 733, King Edward VII Memorial Temperance. As a young man and a patriot he had trained with the old Ulster Volunteer Force (U.V.F. – this was not the same as the loyalist paramilitary group that was formed in 1966) in what was once the Brewery buildings in the heart of Sandy Row. He was a small man with an athletic figure and a progressive outlook to life, as is witnessed by the old photograph given to my mother after his death and which, though yellow with age, depicts him as a young and more than useful left half and founder member of the original Linfield Rangers Football team. A man steeped in the history and tradition of Sandy Row, that Sandy Row, which brought the highest praise regarding its ultra loyalty from no less a personage than William Johnston of Ballykilbeg.

> Oh, Sandy Row! Oh, Sandy Row!
> My Heart is there, where'er I go[1]

Mrs Elizabeth Freeman was a member of the South Belfast Women's Loyal Orange Lodge 17, which celebrated its 100th Anniversary in 2018. A number of the Bridgett sisters, of the famous banner painter William Bridgett & Sons, were in attendance at its first meeting and one of them was Margaret Drennan, who was installed as Worshipful Mistress. There were members from all over Belfast including the Shankill Road, Crumlin Road, Sandy Row, Malone Road and even Andersontown. In 1922 the minute book records that the lodge had 181 members.

Yet as a young lad, I had gone with him to Falls Park, situated deep in the heart of the Republican Falls Road area to romp over that vast expanse of green, not far away from where he and my brother now lie buried under the shadow of Divis Mountain. Often on a Sunday, accompanied by him, I had shared in common with the Roman Catholic children of that district the delights of paddling in

---

[1] Taken from a poem written by the Rev. Dr. Thomas Drew, the rector of Christ Church, Belfast. He read the poem at many public meetings including an Orange Rally in packed Ulster Hall of 5,000 persons on 5th June 1867.

the little stream that still flows through the park, and felt at one with them as I watched them splash and play in the pool. When he took me with him on those Sunday walks, Belfast was his parish just as civil and religious liberty for all was the dominating principle upon which he based his life. He respected the dignity of every man irrespective of his class or creed. Yet he was not a weak man. I remember him taking a shop assistant to task for ignoring him and my younger sister in preference for one of the 'fur coat brigade'. Before he left the shop, he left the shop assistant in no doubt that clothes don't necessarily make the man or woman.

At the conclusion of the thirties, our home had already earned a reputation for its hospitality from many of those inmates and ex-inmates of that grim institute known as the Workhouse. My father often referred to it as the Grubber, also commonly known as the Union and, later, the Welfare, before it was taken over by the Belfast City Hospital. Our house was an ever open door for all (irrespective of where they hung their cap on a Sunday). From all parts of Belfast and further afield they came, the misfit, the misunderstood, the down and out and those who were simply just hungry. From my father, they were always assured of a sympathetic hearing, some practical help if at all possible, and few left without some replenishment to the inner man. Big Lil saw to that.

Quite often when a knock would come to our door at No. 12, the scene was set for the following typical encounter. On answering, that the caller was seeking my father usually became apparent even before any dialogue took place. The drab grey heavy uniform complete with sturdy boots, and the collarless shirt hidden by a grubby silk scarf, all told their own story and marked the caller out as an inmate from the Grubber. 'Is Davie in?' Provided the caller wasn't under the influence, and few ever dared to arrive at our house in such a state, he was ushered in. After a short exchange of greetings my father always got straight to the point. 'Well, what's the matter, Paddy?' The evolving story always took a familiar pattern; he was allowed out to visit friends but Paddy returned back late the previous evening slightly the worse for the drink and been refused admission. After tea was duly served out by Big Lil my father extracted a promise that it wouldn't happen again. (How often had I heard those oft-repeated promises.) Then he would put on his coat and, though he was off duty, made straight up to the Gate Lodge of the Grubber to successfully plead the case for the offender.

But the most interesting memories I possess of the 'good old bad days' belong to the social visits paid to my father from the inmates of the Grubber. For special visits, like those from Wee Barney, who was an inmate and a dwarf with the jolliest laugh I have ever heard for a man of his size, and Jimmy Griffin who sadly spent most of his life between the St. Vincent de Paul's Hostel and the Grubber, Big Lil served a fry. On a sunny summer's evening, the atmosphere for me was terrific, as cigarettes were exchanged and the kitchen filled with the mixture of pipe smoke mingled with that of Woodbine and Park Drive. My father was a confirmed Woodbine and Park Drive smoker. I sat captivated, watching the smoke spiralling up through the rays of the sun streaming in through the windows. The combined odours of tobacco smoke and fry with the smell of phosphorus from the constantly struck matches (Barney's pipe was always going out) will always be one of my fondest memories of No. 12, no less so than the antics of the occupants inside. How my father laughed at Jimmy and Barney both on their feet, in a supposed boxing clinch with Jimmy giving a demonstration of how Tug Boat Wilson bit his poor opponent on the neck in a clinch, with the referee totally unaware of the reasons for his howls of pain. Then to football and my father might give a demonstration of Marshall McEwan pretending to run with the ball to the bewilderment of the fullback who hadn't realized he didn't have the ball with him. Next, it would be Barney's turn, and our kitchen in his imagination became Grosvenor Park and Barney would show us how Johnny Bovril brought the ball to the byline on his frequent trips up the wing. And names from yesteryear, like ghosts from the dim and distant past, once more were clothed in flesh and blood and breathed again in the sanctity of our Sandy Row home. Sam Langford the Boston Tar Baby, Jim Driscoll, Jack Johnston, Touser Crone and Billy McCracken, the list went on and on. In our home, in those days, there were shared memories from both sides of the religious divide, a divide across which hands were to reach out to me on different occasions when as a young man in my teens I suffered from a serious illness.

I can still remember the tenderness and warm embrace of the young Roman Catholic doctor as she put her arms around me so reassuringly and the Roman Catholic ward doctor and sister who nursed me back to health and strength again. These found parallels for me in our little kitchen at No. 12, a sort of haven for many on their way to and from the Grubber. Sandy Row was a good place to live and die in; her sons spoke her name with a feeling of pride and belonging, with no less feeling and conviction than St. Paul, who wherever he went felt proud of his Roman citizenship. Sandy Row offered its sons a common identity with all that was best in our Ulster heritage.

The thirties' swan song found us involved in a second World War, a war which was destined to change the lifestyles and attitudes of many before its final consummation. In contrast, life for the inmates in the Workhouse, ordained from the days when such institutions sprang up all over Ireland to meet the terrible holocaust of the Potato Famine, remained more or less unaffected. There were still the sick, the lame and the lazy and, of course, the able-bodied. The latter were encouraged to carry out tasks about the Work-house for the princely sum of a few ounces of tobacco a week, which I was often called upon to purchase for my father at Ma Carroll's shop. On one such errand it was for chewing tobacco. Even after all these years the words still carry with them the adverse association formed in my mind with the colour yellow. Chewing tobacco! My mind boggled by the possibilities all the way there and part of the way back. Now I had often experienced the smoking of cinnamon stick and when I had felt so inclined, even ate it. But chewing tobacco? Did you chew it before or after you smoked it? Either way, it didn't make sense. It had not gone unnoticed by me that added to the twist of tobacco already on the scales put there by Ma Carroll to make the correct weight, was just the tiniest of pieces. Too insignificant to be missed, but large enough, I felt sure, to satisfy my mounting curiosity. On examination it certainly didn't look anything like liquorice stick, and it had a decidedly peculiar smell, but if it was for chewing, what the odds! Despite its vile taste, I persisted right to the bitter end, always hopeful that my taste buds would suddenly find some justification for its reputed chewing qualities. In the end, the only conclusion I came to was that adults seemed to have an odd sense of values and tastes. All the while I reasoned thus, and I was conscious that my immediate surroundings appeared to be dominated by a brilliant and ghastly yellow. The buildings at our street corner which housed Craig's the grocers and Jackson the window blind shop had just received a facelift of a bright yellow, even Ma Carroll's sported the same colour, not as recently applied and slightly sickly looking to be sure, but still yellow. All this registered on my senses at the same time as my whole gastric system commenced to feel at one with the colourful decor under which I was about to become violently sick. This was borne out on my arrival home by Big Lil who, rather alarmed at my appearance, was quite convinced that I had got jaundice, indeed I probably looked yellow and, if it is at all possible, I felt yellow. My wretched condition was hardly alleviated by the two large tablespoonfuls of castor oil forced down my gullet while Big Lil held my nose, completely ignorant, I may say, as to the cause of my illness.

We lived our lives devoid of many of the social status symbols which for good or ill make up modern society. Cars and taxis were luxuries seldom seen on the streets of my childhood, the exception rather than the rule. A car owner in our district was a rarity and a parked car a curiosity, and usually seen as a forerunner of ill tidings, which in most instances it was, far more often than not it belonged to the local G.P. Planning holidays never interfered with our social activities. The only glimpse of the sea experienced by many came from the generosity of such organizations as Maguire's Sunday School Trip, run by the Methodists from the Grosvenor Hall. Yet totally out of the blue we found ourselves involved in a holiday experience complete with all the trimmings. Unexpectedly, my father and mother and I were invited to spend a few days at Donaghadee, in a house rented for two weeks by a friend of my father's. The excitement was almost unbearable as Big Lil prepared us for the holiday of a lifetime. But all was not yet revealed. My two brothers (my father was married twice, his previous wife had died from tuberculosis) had secretly ordered a taxi. In such unheard of style it arrived in our street, speeding over the square sets and tramway lines (the bottom of our street housed the local tramway depot for our side of Belfast), stopping outside our door to the amazement of my father and the embarrassment of the driver, who had great difficulty persuading my father that he wasn't drunk and hadn't arrived on the wrong street. Eventually, after fervent protestations from my father and amid healthy and vociferous amusement from the many neighbours who had gathered to see 'Wee Davie' (as my father was affectionately known) leave the street in such grandeur, we were bundled into the taxi. But all was not over. The neighbours' amusement heightened, and my father's embarrassment deepened as everyone became aware of the Union Jack proudly flying in the breeze, hastily erected by my two brothers from the upstairs window of our home. When I gazed out at it from the taxi window, I was unaware then that it was for my two brothers a symbol representing an event utterly foreign to our everyday pattern of living, indeed a red-letter day and a good reason for putting the flag out.

14

Pain and tragedy, that grim duo that stalks hand in hand through every Shakespearean drama like a Romeo and Juliet or an Antony and Cleopatra, were also no strangers to the working class people of those days, respecting no barrier of race or creed. But our parents of a bygone age knew what the stuff of life was all about. Treacle bread, potato oaten and shin soup on a Sunday were good for the body, but there was a higher source of energy to be tapped. At the close of the day with the inspiration of his family around him in health and high spirits, a man could hold his head up high knowing that life was worth the living. How often had I heard my father counsel my mother as she gave way to tears in the constant struggle to make ends meet; pointing out to her that the important things are those which money can't buy, and this fact has never been the monopoly of any one class. Then with quiet dignity, he would say, 'Lil, if you don't stop your crying you'll leave yourself open for something really serious to cry about.' And things can never go badly wrong if the heart be true and the love be strong, for when the storms come, then the weeping rain will be changed by love into the sunshine again.

My mother, unlike my father and I, was not Sandy Row born and bred, but came from Carnaughliss, Ballyhill, and met my father in the course of their employment and so Sandy Row became my mother's by adoption when my father took her as his young bride to live at No. 12. Big Lil was a country girl, but none the worse for that, a good-looker, good cook and a loving wife to her husband. Nature had endowed her with remarkable health and courage. Her sandy hair to the admiration of her friends, who came to regard her as having been blessed with eternal youth, defied the years of stress and strain. Many a time over the years I had heard a neighbour's exclamation to my father: 'Lizzie never seems to change.' She was completely dependent on my father and just as devoted. This was no more obvious than when she came to share his humble home. The newly-weds' first task at No. 12 was to extract the many nails which literally covered the walls and ceilings, hammered in for reasons known only to the mind of the previous tenant.

Our home was typical of most in those days of mounting unemployment. Its main odours were those of candle grease and Sunlight soap. For lighting in our bedrooms, we relied upon a candle. The luxury of gas was reserved for our kitchen centrepiece which was a large range fire complete with oven, hobs and fender, all of which my mother vigorously blackleaded daily. Sparse oilcloth covered our kitchen floor, ending at walls painted in two-tone: the bottom half brown and top half green. The light streaming into our kitchen was broken up by the many tiny window panes which made up our window; twelve in all, each surrounded by a wooden frame. Our precious items of furniture consisted mainly of two wooden railed chairs, a stool and a large black and sombre-looking Victorian sideboard (I think the sofa came later), and a large wooden table scrubbed daily with Sunlight soap, and under which I spent many happy hours with a candle, carefully leaving for posterity my name turned in various designs on the underpart of the tabletop.

Our scullery was hidden from the kitchen by a huge door which opened and closed on an elaborate latch mechanism and seemed more befitting on an outside entry rather than a pantry door. Inside, a huge stone Jawbox sink, erected in such a way that it appeared to be suspended in mid-air, accounted for most of our personal hygiene and was the only object to relieve the otherwise unbroken monotony and boredom of our small scullery.

All Big Lil's cooking was carried out on a single gas ring connected to a tube in the corner of our kitchen, and from its dangerous jets tragedy was to strike. In an unguarded moment, her long dress was exposed to the naked flame of the gas ring and her young body enveloped in flames. In a state of shock, she ran screaming into our street and the fresh oxygen further fed the flames. Mercifully, she was met by kind friends and quick-thinking neighbours who ministered to her in her dire plight. Though too young to understand all that had happened, I was not likely to forget my first separation from Big Lil and the ambulance whisking her away as it departed out of our street. 'Weeping may endure for a night, but joy cometh in the morning'[2] and with youth and health on her side, Big Lil was soon to return to us again,

---

[2] Psalm 30:5.

unscathed and apparently none the worse for her trying ordeal.

'The good old days', was an emotive description of the past my father refused to allow himself to be identified with. His more apt rephrase 'The good old bad days' was, I believe, a more accurate description and a genuine attempt by him of a rational and balanced reflection of past events seen as a triumph of human dignity in spite of existing social evils. Probably his was also an ambivalent attitude, but certainly, he was never guilty of looking at the past through rose-coloured spectacles. Yet I believe there existed in those days a resilience which encouraged a more positive outlook on life; an ability to look for the silver lining. Not just an acceptance of one's lot, but a determination to carry on regardless and to smile in the face of adversity and mishap. One such occasion arose in our family circle, bringing in its wake merriment out of apparent calamity.

Big Lil's young sister had left behind the security of a rural existence with all its fresh air, open fields and simplicity for the turbulence of the big smoke. In the pressures of survival synonymous with city life, she had fallen into ill health and was admitted to Whiteabbey Sanatorium. On hearing the news, Big Lil wasn't long in making arrangements to see her sister. Life was simple in those days, and even the short journey to Whiteabbey was not without its complications and required a great deal of preparation for such a venture.

Wednesday was visiting day. Well in advance Big Lil prepared the goodies consisting of lemonade, home-baked apple tart, (which was the envy of many in our district) and some fresh oranges. There had been last-minute hitches. Consequently, the morning of departure found Big Lil busily engaged in finishing off her washing. The washboard gave off its own peculiar rhythm as her powerful arms plunged the sheets in and out of the bathtub and along the ribs of the half-submerged washboard. Many an evening I had sat fascinated as I watched her perform her wash duties, mystified when a warm coal fell from the grate to see her lift it in her bare hands and return it to the fire. Even after all these years I can still not compete with her on that score.

The washing completed, the clock on the shelf indicated it was time to be off. Hastily she gathered her precious goodies. A mere toddler, I was not allowed to go with her, the risk would be too great. Stepping out into our street, she made her departure, but not before well-intentioned neighbours contributed to her delay. 'Well Lil, are you off to see your sister? Tell her we were all asking about her.' Meanwhile, the precious moments slipped by unheeded as she answered many questions regarding her sister. She was finally at the tram stop and, realizing now the necessity for speed, the tram could not come quickly enough for her.

Eventually, the L.M.S. Railway loomed into view. Alighting from the tram, she made straight for the railway and ticket office. In her haste she handed over the price of a single ticket, gasping out, 'Whiteabbey Hospital, please.' The ticket clerk mused as he looked at the money handed over to him and from that to the young woman in front of him. Next, he leaned out of the small aperture of the ticket cubicle (somewhat like an overzealous clock cuckoo), taking in as he did so a more detailed observation of the anxious figure in front of him (a figure that glowed with health and vitality from the crown of her sandy hair to the tip of her toes). 'I take it you'll be coming back?' he enquired. In reply, Big Lil fumbled in her handbag and all the while the precious seconds were flying by. It was now two o'clock, the time for her train. Somewhere in the station, as if to bring home to her a renewed sense of urgency, a train suddenly released a jet of steam into the air with an accompanying whistle, signalling its impatience to be gone. At last the required money passed over the counter and the return ticket was purchased, but what platform? In the confusion over the little drama enacted over the tickets, she wasn't sure. On reflection, she realized it could have been Platform 5 but still it must be 4, and at Platform 4 she arrived. The guard was busily engaged in exercising his tonsils in the best Belfast manner: 'Come on there, or I will be late.'

Big Lil didn't need a second invite and she was carried along in the heaving and pushing of the crowd, she was swept past a somewhat disgruntled ticket collector who, furious at this belated activity, kept insisting for some reason or other that women, in general, could be relied upon to be late even for their own funeral. The waiting train was not unaffected by all this disparagement of womanhood as it rocked back and then forward between the shunters, as if announcing to all and sundry its anxiety to be off.

Big Lil eased herself into the cushion seats on the corridor train, clutching her prepared goodies as she did so. No carriage rack for them, the constant feel of their nearness somehow brought with it an assurance of their safety. The only other occupant of the carriage was an elderly and well-dressed gentleman. With a jolt the train started, soon the dreary back streets of Belfast were but a memory as they raced further and further out into the open country and into a setting, which brought nostalgic reminiscences to Big Lil of early childhood days only temporarily forgotten. But all was not well at the back of Big Lil's mind. Something was ill at ease. The sentinel guarding the unconscious area of her mind against the conscious seemed to be trying to impart some message to her. She was definitely uneasy, almost uncomfortable, while the message clear and distinct if not highly informative (except for those that have an ear for such things) rang out loud and clear, as the aggravated sound of the wheel upon the track rose and fell in a mounting crescendo of unyielding resistance, whining as it went, 'You shouldn't be here! You shouldn't be here!'

On and on thundered the train as it puffed along to the rhythm of R. L. Stevenson's poem 'Faster than fairies, faster than witches, | Bridges and houses, hedges and ditches.' Indeed, soon whole railway stations seemed to materialize but for a moment and then disappear into apparent obscurity. But Big Lil was tired. The last-minute washing, the preparation and the excitement added to the quietness in the carriage (not a sound had uttered forth from the old boy so engrossed was he in his reading) and the gentle rocking motion of the carriage created within her tired body the impression of being nursed in a giant womb. Soon she was fast asleep. She awoke with a start, the carriage had been invaded, the quietness violated as youngsters clamouring with excitement, wielding their buckets and spades, poured into the carriage, brushing past her, each anxious to catch a glimpse of the sea. Then, with a whoop of delight, they were away again beating their spades upon their buckets as they disappeared down the corridors of the train. Now the sentinel was really doing its work. She became alarmed. Whiteabbey Hospital, buckets and spades and a child's unbridled enthusiasm for the sea? Somehow the pattern did not fit. Pulling herself together and in a hollow voice she stammered out (addressing herself to the well-dressed gentleman), 'Will we be arriving soon at Whiteabbey Station?' What seemed a lifetime passed before the old gentleman was able to answer. Then, having recovered from the initial shock of the question, in the most sympathetic mannerism which he could muster, he replied, 'Whiteabbey did you say? Dear lady, our next stop I am afraid will be Portrush, all of fifty miles past your intended destination.' Big Lil's fears were suddenly, realized. In her excitement, she had boarded the Holiday Express, a non-stop train for Portrush.

In our home at No. 12, many anxious moments passed into hours at the non-arrival of Big Lil. All sorts of conjectures were put forth by my father and brothers as to the reason for her delay. Perhaps her sister had taken a turn for the worse? Surely she couldn't be talking to some enquiring neighbour all this time? Repeated trips to the door brought no sign of her. In the growing dusk, she arrived home, tired and bedraggled, her eyes still red from many a tear shed on the long journey home. However, round our well-scrubbed table, amidst the hysterical laughter of my father and brothers (and joined in by Big Lil – they never let her forget it), with a word of sympathy and a cup of tea, we helped her finish off the goodies.

Trams arriving and departing from the tram depot made Gaffikin Street, one of Belfast's busiest streets. Despite many children playing in the street, the accident rate involving them was practically nil. Sandy Row Orange Hall can be seen at the end of the street.

Chapter 2

Childhood Memories

My earliest childhood memories that spring most readily to mind form a somewhat mixed bag of totally unrelated events like: 'Little Sir Echo' blaring out from some old-fashioned gramophone somewhere about the Row; the soft Popeye-type sailor doll which, immediately before retiring for bed, I carefully put to sleep each night; my fascination for the brass beehive-shaped bell that sat on the table in some hallways in the district; the sense of embarrassment and intrusion of privacy which I had later felt when as a toddler I followed Big Lil into a neighbour's house, just as the poor woman was caught up in the final stages of giving birth; Cissy's rousing and bawdy exclamation on discovering the motives for my sudden rolling about on the floor as she caught me unashamedly manoeuvring myself into a position where I could look up her long dress to see where her legs went to.

My step-brother Jim, I did not know. My only knowledge of him came through photographs, and letters exchanged between him and my father. Seeking employment, he had departed for England and did not return again for many years. It was not until after the war, therefore, that I was able to establish any form of relationship with him. Not so my other brother Davie, he was my friend and hero. I worshipped him with all the wonder and innocence of boyhood. When he gathered, as was the custom then, along with the boys at the corner outside Bobby Gardiner's shop, he cut a slim and attractive figure, clad in his smart grey suit and sporting a fashionable rubber belt on the silver buckle of which was inscribed the letter 'D'. At five years of age, I eagerly paraded around our small backyard after him, marching proudly behind him to the skirl of the pipes while he practised as a young piper and member of the Prince of Wales Band. At eighteen, and almost before the first shot was fired in anger, he had exchanged one uniform for another. Some of his courage and charm is still to be seen, captured in the old photograph of him in naval uniform which hangs in No. 12, adorning one side of our chimney breast. On the opposite side hangs his obituary in the form of a scroll. With only eighteen years' experience of real living behind him, I suppose he could have had no other.

This scroll commemorates AB Seaman D. Freeman
Held in Honour as one who Served King and
Country In the World War of 1939–1945
And gave his life to save Mankind from Tyranny
May his Sacrifice help to Bring about the Peace and
Freedom for which he died.

After the war ground to a halt, he was to die, and his wife
and baby son were housed in a Nissen hut in Sydenham. My
own attempts to recall the circumstances surrounding my
brother's departure to the war is somewhat sketchy in parts,
like an unfinished watercolour, on which the artist has applied his colours to the more essential details only. But the
highlights stand out clearly and unmistakably. I can still see
my brother as he stood in the middle of our kitchen, clad in
the long black oilskin that covered his naval uniform. He
made his last farewells to the little family group assembled
there – outside it was blowing a gale. Inside the atmosphere
was dark and foreboding, conflicting emotions like sadness
and pride were the order of the evening. It had only been a
few months previous since my brother Jim, unable to find
suitable employment, instructed my father in the following
course of action if he did not return by a specific time that
evening. He was to lock the door, and my brother would
correspond with him later, as he did – from London. Now
here was 'Wee Davie', the spitting image of his father and
him so young, committed to serving his King and Country.

There was sadness but a strong sense of pride also, that same feeling of pride that possessed my father in the later years of the war, when turning to my mother he would often say, 'Our Davie had never served an hour late and met each termination of his leave without a word of complaint.' Quietly they waited as a family met together for the last time for a long while to come.

Ears cocked as they listened for the knock on the door which would tell them that Davie's pals from schoolboy days had arrived for him. As boys, they had played together on the streets of Sandy Row. Now they would answer their country's call together. Our street in common with many in Sandy Row had not been reluctant when the time came to give of her sons. One had gone down with the *Hood*, others also made the supreme sacrifice.

> For some we loved, the loveliest and the best
> That from his Vintage rolling Time hath prest,
> Have drunk their Cup a Round or two before,
> And one by one crept silently to rest,

My brother's departure gave vent to an artistic trait in me, which unfortunately, let me hasten to add, did not progress to any great heights. Each time my parents wrote to him, enclosed with their letter was my own personal correspondence to him. My own version of what the war was all about, as seen through the eyes of a five-year-old. From his replies to my parents I learnt that my cryptic messages gave his shipmates a great deal of pleasure and amusement. A typical letter of mine began with a drawing of a very obviously British ship steaming ahead with all flags flying. Three funnels belched out smoke while six-inch guns blazed away, poking their heads out from every conceivable angle. The sky above was generally plastered with flak and quite a few German planes were well on their way to Davy Jones's Locker. Next came a drawing of Davie complete with a naval cap on which I had printed the name of his ship. These 'hieroglyphics' usually ended with a very good drawing of a skull and crossbones and printed exhortations about bringing the war to a speedy close.

Workman School set in the heart of the loyalist Sandy Row was the school I attended, and a fitting school at that for a loyal son of the Row to belong. Situated among streets whose very names were constant reminders to us of our glorious heritage, it was flanked by Boyne Street on one side and Aughrim Street on the other. The most direct approach to the school, coming in off Sandy Row, was by Schomberg Street, named in honour of King William's faithful General. It was here that I was first initiated in the three Rs and round it, in my infancy, with indeed no reflection on the school, grew all my childhood fears and fantasies. The umbilical cord which had at birth made me one with my mother threatened to strangle me; I just refused to be parted, and so school age came and went and still for one reason or another my schooling was delayed.

At the manly age of six and over I was marched round to school where my first encounter with Miss Tate was destined to end in disaster. We viewed ourselves in the manner of potential opponents before hostilities have begun. I was quite certain when she looked me over on our first meeting that I detected a distinct look of disapproval, particularly as she watched me squirm behind my mother's protective figure. Her opening remarks were anything but reassuring. 'And what do you call him?' she enquired of my mother. On receiving the required information, she turned to me: 'Come along boy.' At this brusque invitation, I left my mother behind and with a heavy heart and grave misgivings I soon found myself unceremoniously ushered into the classroom. Into a world of strange faces and unfamiliar smells and sounds, like the ever increasing but completely ignored sound of the baby delinquent, who having battered his piece of plasticine into a thousand and one dubious shapes decides that school and adult supervision has nothing more to offer him. This was a traumatic experience I had already decided to spare myself, something to be avoided at all costs if at all possible, and so much was the speed of my next course of action that I can say, on reflection, I took everyone completely by surprise, including the capable Miss Tate. Meanwhile, my mother, having safely handed over her firstborn, turned her back on the school and made for home, probably chatting to a neighbour on the way. That morning there were chores to be finished, so she arrived at No. 12 with the minimum of delay. She could hardly believe her eyes as the door was opened for standing in the middle of the kitchen complete with a school bag, was yours truly. A state of shock momentarily set in and then she sprang into action and I was frogmarched back to school again to face the wrath of Miss Tate.

The reception I got was quite inhospitable, to say the least. 'You bad little pill,' she screamed. This I was to learn was one of her favourite expressions of disapproval. While I was in her class, I always had the impression that my latest escapade had confirmed her worst suspicions of me. At six years of age and over I was an overgrown baby. Any mistake on my part in those infancy days was taken as confirmation of this. Holding my book up in class in front of all and sundry (I was unfortunate enough to have put the figure three the wrong way round) she cried out to everyone, 'Look at the wee baby, he can't even make a three.' I had got off to a bad start. I had challenged and indeed flouted the authority of the school. By my actions, my manhood (or should it be boyhood?) had been rightly regarded as suspect. It was not a happy time for me and probably less so for the school.

The Clinic was a medical body ordained by the authorities to meet the many and varied elements of those schoolchildren from all over Belfast who by necessity resorted there. It was a depressing place to visit, a guaranteed, never-to-be-forgotten experience. During the waiting time, it never failed to alarm me to hear our afflictions, ranging in severity from impetigo to scarlet fever, so openly discussed and freely commented on by those gathered there. I detested my visits there but saw them as a means to an end, a further stay of execution, with a sick line covering in some cases two to six weeks. What the doctors diagnosed on my many visits I am unable to recall, except to state that I generally ended up with a sick line and a large jar of Radio Malt, which was faithfully spooned into me following the directions given.

The only ray of sunshine in my drab and inconspicuous if not entirely uneventful schooling, indeed the only thing I feel that justified the whole school system, was the singing lessons, conducted by Miss Barr. We had generally gone through the 'Jolly Sailor Boys' and 'Bobby Shafto' when Miss Barr, with a mischievous twinkle in her eye, would ask if there was any other song we felt inclined to sing. The response was always overwhelming, thus as in every singing lesson we arrived at the singing of our favourite, 'Billy Boy'. Miss Barr involved herself in this piece with unusual enthusiasm, her tuning fork working overtime as it bobbed about in mid-air to the sound of our singing as if it were creating whimsical crotchets and semiquavers. I always watched her face intently, waiting for the change that slowly crept across it during our response to the singing of the chorus:

> Oh my Nancy tickle my fancy
> Oh my charming, Billy Boy.

It seemed to me at this juncture of the stanza that Miss Barr, with puckered lips and that 'Oh, you are awful!' expression, was rightly interpreting our response of muffled titters gradually reaching a crescendo of uncontrollable laughter, as an inability on our part at this stage of our education to accept the idea of someone's fancy being tickled without feeling that it referred to some unmentionable part of the human anatomy.

A school bag was not the only essential part of our equipment; along with such extras as penknives, string and marbles, the usual stock-in-trade of most schoolboys, we had to carry our gas masks with us wherever we went, at least so we were told. They were a constant reminder to us, apart from rationing of course, that Europe was in the grip of a deadly war. Even our cigarette cards carried detailed instructions and illustrations on how to deal with an incendiary bomb.

Some of the priorities of the Propaganda War were rather confusing to a boy who had already blown many Jerry planes to kingdom come on his school jotter. 'Dig for Victory', we were extolled. How could an army, even with the best will in the world, equipped with small spades even hope to defeat the Germans? 'Careless talk costs lives': what had talking to do with winning the war? Miss Tate was an aggressive talker; I often thought that she could make the enemy run, but then not everyone was gifted to the same extent as Miss Tate. 'Walls have ears' - this was a real mind bender. I often wondered if this was some new and sinister German invention of which we had to beware. For any young lad with the least spark of imagination, they were fascinating times in which to live, yet as young boys, we were not too preoccupied with thoughts of the war. At this early stage of its development, we were inclined to think of it as the war that was over there in Europe. For most of us, life in Sandy Row went on more or less as normal apart from those, of course, whose dads had gone off to fight in the war.

Our community activities and social institutions remained somewhat unchanged and, of course, the streets still echoed to the many and exciting cries of that colourful band of street traders who plied their many wares about our streets. In many ways, their presence among us brought a sense of stability, a realization that life must go on. They each came, it seemed, at their appointed time, just as the seasons promised in the Bible. On wash day it was the ragman from the Pound Loney. He never passed our door without shouting in, 'Any rags, Missus? Some nice cups for rags, Missus.' My mother was usually busy when he called and came to the door in answer to his call complete with pinny and smoothing back her long hair from her forehead. 'Sure, I'll call back again in another ten minutes, and you'll have something ready for me.' And at the appointed time almost like Cinderella at the ball, the rags turned into riches, and our kitchen utensils would be further added to. On his departure from our door I would often watch him with a ragbag swung over his shoulder as he headed for his cart further down our street. On it was gathered the most intriguing and gaily assorted bits and pieces that any young boy in his wildest dreams could ever hope to encounter. But it was the balloons that captivated me, balloons of every shape, size and colour, so many in fact, that when I watched them all straining and swaying in the breeze it was easy for me to identify his cart with the magic carpet I had so often followed spellbound in the films as it floated over the kingdom of some eastern potentate. Only the magic carpet became a rag man's cart whisked on high by the breeze and drifting over Sandy Row, carried into the sky by the many gaily coloured balloons which hung from it. On arrival at his cart, the ragbag was promptly emptied, the wicker basket of dishes carefully positioned on the cart, and then with a push and a heave between the shafts he continued on down our street advertising his requirements as he went. 'Rags, jam pots and bottles!' This always sent me scurrying back home to Big Lil for a jam pot in exchange for which I was always sure of owning one of those coveted balloons on a stick.

On Sunday it was the turn of Fusco the ice cream man, pushing his red painted cart on what looked like two huge cartwheels. He was probably the most popular of all. There was no mistaking his arrival in our street. The placing of a battered and well-worn bugle to his lips sent the clarion call out loud and clear. It always reminded me of the type used

35

in some Custer film to regroup the cavalry in the face of the advancing Indians. On a warm Sunday afternoon, it had a similar effect on us. It was a morale booster as off we scampered to plead our case for a penny poke, to parents already well prepared for our arrival. Our objective accomplished, we descended on the Fusco (to use the same analogy) like a horde all clamouring for attention. Standing at his cart, my penny clutched in my hand, I completely identified myself with the ritual being enacted in front of my transfixed eyes. One swarthy arm would systematically dive into the depths of the ice cream cart, while the other hovered above like the sword of Damocles beheading any surplus ice cream which went falling back into the cart. Deftly he would smooth the ice cream into shape and then, for me the most important part of all, an anticipated liberal sprinkling of raspberry sauce on top. This came from a bottle similar to the one Blake the Sandy Row barber used for his final hairdressing, short and squat with tiny holes puncturing its top and full of that precious red liquid. This dressing was the final moment of ecstasy. I always watched intently till this part of the ritual was carried out. For after all it had not been unknown for him to have missed out and push an undressed cone into the hands of an unsuspecting recipient; what a sacrilege!

A touch of humour was added to the scene by the appearance of a certain individual who religiously answered the Clarion call and in so doing gave a great deal of amusement to those assembled there, with subsequent embarrassment to the ice cream vendor. Some said this was brought about by a slight impediment in his speech, others felt that the young lad had been deliberately misinformed as to Fusco's correct name. I suspected the latter. If there was a slight defect in his speech, there was certainly nothing wrong with his lungs and to hear him shout Fusco's name that sounded like a common swear word at the top of his voice was quite startling and a definite breach of the Sabbath in any language.

Even our bread arrived surrounded by a certain amount of drama and excitement, as the large iron-rimmed wheels of the bread cart rumbled over the square sets, now and then sending sparks showering into the air as they came in contact with the grooves of the tramway line. The poor horse struggled to regain its authority over the situation as the tramway lines threatened to take her on their own particular course. Often I had watched in admiration as Milligan, our bread man, perched perilously high on the top of his cart, with great skill and a flick of the long whip and a sharp pull on the reins, brought the frightened animal under control. For reasons best known to mischievous boys we would watch intently while he dismounted and halted his bread cart at a strategic position in our street. He would deal with the customers as they came, call on others with the usual, and seek out those whose needs the previous week had been greater than their income allowed. Then with his last position reached and his business in our street transacted, he would mount his cart in preparation for his journey into the next street. This was the moment for which Jackie and I waited. Almost as one, we raced for the cart, while each of us, in turn, tried to outdo the other clinging tenaciously to the two handles on the back doors as we were lifted into the air by the rocking motion of the cart. Up and down we went; it was the thrill of a lifetime. But Milligan, pushed further into the air by the added weight on the springs at the back, knew he had picked up an uninvited passenger or two. Wholly unruffled and to all intents and purposes unaware of what was going on, he would raise his whip as if to spur the horse on to greater efforts. Then a sudden backward flick of the wrist sent the long whip cracking and curling dangerously close to our heads. Even at that tender age the message was clear, it was time for us to part from Milligan and his cart. Although bent on mischief it was the only reaction we ever got from him, nothing verbal, just a flick of the wrist was enough to bring about the desired result, our departure.

From Milligan, as if by some relationship of opposites, we usually turned our attention to the man on duty at the entrance to the tramway depot. All that we required there were a few catcalls to draw attention to ourselves (at a safe distance of course) and then a brief imitation of his gammy leg. Jackie was an expert at copying his up and down gait.[3] What followed after this was entirely predictable, to our howls of wild delight, like a man possessed, he pursued us relentlessly from one street to another. Jackie was sometimes my rival, but always my closest friend in every sense of the word. We lived only a few doors from each other, grew up together, went to the same school and were of similar ages. But the bond that existed between us went much deeper even than that, cemented by the many boyish pranks and jokes and snared peccadillos peculiar to us (we both bit our nails furiously and were obsessed with the conceited notion that each week saw one of us outstrip the other in stature). Consequently the slightest clash of egos, whether brought about by a difference of opinion as to which of us ran the faster, could out wrestle the other, was a funky knuckle at marbles or was the smarter, was resolved when we stood back to back and sought the nearest independent judgement on our latest rise in feet and inches. Yet the ties that bound us went far beyond the vanities of this temporal scene. For many a secret we had shared together. Our lips sealed by an oath made before God, with hands raised on high and which committed us even unto death.

---

[3] Gammy leg, meaning a leg unable to function normally because of injury or chronic pain.

Jackie was the youngest of the male side of his parents' offspring, and after him came two sisters, the only female contributions, making a sum total of six children in all. His father was a carter for Wordies, a well-known firm in Belfast, and his mother, in spite of crippling arthritis, bravely worked out to help supplement the family income. This arrangement was often cruelly taken advantage of, as it enabled Jackie, in his parents' absence, to invite me to share the secrets of his father's wardrobe. Often when we returned from school on a wet afternoon I crept upstairs behind him, deeply conscious of the holy ritual in which I was about to become involved. Once we were in the bedroom, Jackie rummaged among his father's personal belongings until he produced his dad's black bowler, which was always filled with tissue paper to keep its shape conveniently allowing it to sit with some degree of dignity upon my head. Next, he tied around my waist the traditional apron with its sacred symbols worn by his father when he paraded as a member of the Royal Black Preceptory. Though unable to appreciate many of its historical or religious implications we realized it belonged to the traditions of our fathers and forefathers and to wear it was in some mystical way to become part of it. But alas, soon the wonder and sense of awe we associated with our previous trips upstairs became lost to us. And the bowler once so reverently handled was merely improvised of as a prop, used by us to imitate a Laurel and Hardy stunt we had seen at the pictures. Each of us, in turn, would stand back against the wall and face the wardrobe mirror where we would try and outdo the other in making the hat appear to rise unaided above our heads. This was achieved by merely leaning, backwards and squeezing the rim of the hat against the wall. The feeling of accomplishment produced by these antics of ours was terrific, but the poor hat suffered in consequence. So much, in fact, that on one of our trips we discovered it had been removed. Apparently, someone had decided that fair wear and tear couldn't account for its apparent battered condition.

Quite often, when we couldn't be located upstairs, it was safely assumed that we had scaled the railway wall and were on the embankment. Here, under closest secrecy and in the growing dusk, we hid for the benefit of future generations some of those items most dear to us. After having carefully measured the spot by the width of our strides, we would select the place, dig a hole and empty our pockets. What treasures ushered forth. One such collection of ours was a chestnut (or a cheeser, as we called them) reputed to be cock over a hundred others(this was Jackie's main contribution), while I parted with a trick nail bent in a U shape in the middle and which when slipped between the fingers gave the impression that one of them was impaled. Tramway tickets, an army button, a selection of coloured bottle tops and a half a box of Bengal matches followed and, as a sort of benediction pronounced on all that had gone before, I slipped in one of the Big Lil's apostle spoons. I thought she would under-stand. Funny though, when all was revealed after the discov-ery of its absence she could not see any spiritual connection at all.

Beyond the railway embankment were the streets. They were ours; they belonged to us. For it was on them and from them that we played and devised the many games that kept us out of mischief during the long clear nights of summer. Most of the games we played were a legacy left to us from the past. They were timeless, belonging to no particular gen-eration or locality. Games like Iron Tig which with the tramway lines was an obvious one for us. Then there were others like, Rallo, Eggo, Thunder and Lightning, Rounders and my favourite game which we called Churchey One Over. Improvisation was the name of the game in those days and cigarette cards dropped from a windowsill, or placed in the confines of a flagstone and attacked with a tennis ball, gave us hours of pleasure and enjoyment. Even the pubs (and there was no shortage of them) supplied us with any amount of tin tops which with a little ingenuity found their way onto our jerseys; worn by taking out the cork backing and with a little pressure sandwiching one's jersey between it and the inside of the tin top.

'He's a great lad with a hanky ball,' was a comment often used derisively as a reluctant recognition of ability and tal-ent. It is a comment probably meaningless to our present generation, but the once famous hanky ball from which this saying arose was more than just a substitute for the real thing. In its own right, it had become a popular and accepted object of play. It was not the first time Jackie and I had kicked our hanky ball long into the evening, until in the flickering shadows cast by the street gas lamps we were unable to follow its flight any longer as we propelled it from one to the other. For the uninformed, our hanky ball consisted of old newspapers tightly squeezed into the shape of a ball and covered by a handkerchief or old rag.

Hopscotch, skipping, swinging on the lamps, peeries and whips and such games each appeared spontaneously at their own given time of the year, as if in answer to an overall impulse triggered off by some inbuilt mechanism within the mind of youth. Then there were the games of dare peculiar to our own street and entered into with real gusto by Jackie and me, such as hopping a ride on the trams as they returned to the depot. The object of this game was to remain unnoticed by the conductor and driver and smuggle ourselves into the depot. Once inside we further tested our courage by the dangerous exercise of jumping clear across the tram pits.

Entertainment was mostly of our own making, except of course when it came in such organized forms as the cinema. Jackie and I were its most dedicated adherents. It was the acme of our social life, particularly during the long dark winter evenings. We worshipped at its shrine and for most of us it became a way of life. There were no lengths to which we would not go to spend an evening at the local fleapit. We would chop sticks, run errands, look after the baby and commit ourselves to anything that promised as its final reward the possibility of obtaining the required admission price. It was not just once that my father, as he finished work, was confronted by me at the Grubber gates, pleading my case for the picture money. With the many demands on what little money we had, the necessity to get in first was always uppermost in my mind.

It wasn't often that I missed out, but once when I failed through lack of capital to see Spencer Tracy in *Stanley and Livingstone*, it proved a real disappointment. For only the week previous to this, probably influenced by the usual 'Coming Attractions', I was filled with enthusiasm and admiration for this famous missionary explorer equal to my most youthful imagination. Such was my zeal that, accompanied by Jackie, we went to a favourite haunt of ours in the Botanic Gardens known to us as the puzzle walks. A very impressionable youngster, it was here that I decided to offer up my life on the altar of community service as an explorer. Big Lil's loss was to be the world's gain. Jackie reverently kept watching while with great solemnity and dexterity I chose a large stone for each word of my solemn covenant, five in all, accounting for my avowal that 'I will be an explorer.' Each stone was thrown vigorously into a little pond which was half covered by a cave-like structure; it was the ideal setting amongst the towering plants that surrounded us. However, in my keenness, I had made use of some of the stones forming a part of the rock gardens. The loud splash made by each stone as it entered the water, attracted the attention of Rubber Neck, the park ranger, an efficient and agile gentleman dedicated to the apprehension of all would-be violators of the park's sanctity. To the sound of whistles blowing we made a rather undignified withdrawal from the spot so recently the scene of such spirited self-sacrifice and commitment. Nevertheless, Rubber Neck's pleas for us to hold still a minute while we talked the whole thing over fell on deaf ears. The stick he brandished with its needle-sharp point and which he had no qualms about converting into a handy projectile put paid to that.

I had been unable to see Spencer Tracy in *Stanley and Livingstone*, but I was to be given another opportunity to see him. The months had slipped by, and I had long since learned to live with my disappointment. When to my great excitement I discovered that the Coliseum was proudly presenting, as its coming attraction for the first three days of the incoming week, that popular R. L. Stevenson drama of dual personality, *Dr Jekyll and Mr Hyde*, and starring no less a person than the star actor Spencer Tracy, I was determined to see the film. But the jinx that had dogged my attempts to see *Stanley and Livingstone* seemed to have struck once more. Having, with negative results, exhausted all possibilities for obtaining the money, and with the advent of Wednesday the last day of its showing, it appeared that all was lost when completely out of the blue came the opportunity to run an errand. Big Lil sent for me with the hint that it could be financially rewarding. I was to call with an elderly lady living down our street. In answer to my knock at the door, I was handed a lemonade bottle and nine pence. I was puzzled, what on earth was the bottle for? To my amazement, I learnt that the nine pence was for me. Now I had often received a penny or tuppence for services rendered. Although my mother always insisted that I should never take advantage of any such errands of mercy by 'having recompense unto the reward', I always got around it by sticking out my hand and saying unconvincingly 'No thank you.' But here clutched in my hand was nine pence. I began making quick calculations. I could afford a session downstairs in the Coliseum for six-pence and still, have enough money for a newspaper full of chips. Or in the same cinema, I could treat myself to the luxury of the gods at nine pence, with all the trimmings of cushion seats.

Admission Free – Pay at the Door –
Cushion Seats – Sit on the Floor.

An anxious inquirer soon interrupted my thoughts. 'Do you know the spring at the top of the Whiterock, on Divis Mountain?' Without waiting for an answer, she continued 'Your mother says you do,' which was true, for I had been there at different times with my father. I nodded in reply, wondering what was coming next. To my further surprise, she asked, 'Will you fill that bottle at the spring for me?' As if in answer to my bewilderment she went on, 'It's a good cure for whooping cough.' It was obvious that she had great faith in its medicinal properties. Quickly I started off on my long journey and though long before I had ever heard of the sound wisdom of the eastern proverb relating to Mohammed and the mountain, I soon began to discuss with myself the moral rights and wrongs and possible consequences were I to bring the mountain a little nearer, say into our backyard at No. 12. But fears that without the benefit of this magical potion she might die dismissed from my mind all such thoughts of fetching the water from the closer proximity of Sandy Row. And that evening made it all worthwhile as my mountain ordeal completely forgotten I sat scared out of my pants as I watched the strange forces of good and evil do battle for the soul of Dr Jekyll.

Chapter 3
Picture Halls

These were the days of the long picture queues for it was to be another twenty years at least before television was to supersede the popularity of the picture hall. Indeed as a youngster I had never heard of the smaller version of the silver screen. I listened to programmes on a battery-operated wireless in Scotty's house; he was my second best friend. But television as a commercial commodity belonged to a later generation and the monopoly of a higher social strata long before its antennae graced our packed chimney stacks.

The local cinemas, like their counterparts around the city centre, usually ran a continuous performance from early afternoon right through till 10.30 p.m. or shortly after. Our local Sandy Row halls, and such like, only offered their patrons the choice of two distinct performances each evening, with a complete clearing of the hall after each show, comprising of the first house at shortly after 6 p.m. and the second at 8.30 p.m. Quite often Jackie and I and other adherents took the fullest possible advantage from the continuous performance. This we did by going into halls like the Majestic on the Lisburn Road directly after school and sitting through one complete performance and halfway, as our fancy took us, through the next. When we eventually made our exit carrying school bags, which only drew attention to our early patronage, it was not unknown for us to come under a barrage of verbal abuse and insults, some even casting doubt upon our family progenitors, hurled at us from an exasperated and long-suffering public who had patiently waited in the queue outside. In retaliation, and to everyone's disgust we often revealed the outcome to some of the more intimate moments of the film we had just seen.

Skinny malink melodeon legs
Big Banana Feet, Went to the Pictures
But couldn't get a seat.

In Sandy Row, we were fortunate in that there were some picture halls all within easy reach. Those which I frequented the most, in order of preference, were the Sandro, known locally as the Shack, then there was the Coliseum (or as we knew it in its abbreviated form, the Coll) and the Windsor. Nearer the city centre but still quite convenient was the Kelvin, so named because it was on the former site of Lord Kelvin's house in College Square East.

Admission to the Coliseum in my early days was a token with a hole in it, purchased on entering the cinema and of which I was promptly relieved by an attendant who slid it onto a stick. My favourite was the Shack whose reputation among the locals went back to the days when it had opened forth its doors on presentation of a jam pot. Certainly, I can remember admission prices at 2*d*. for the matinee and 3*d*. for an evening performance. To my boyish nostrils, the powerful odour of the Shack came from industrial disinfectant swilled liberally by Robbie along the rows at the end of each performance, until it gathered in small stagnant pools of white among the rows of wooden forms. Here the pressures of the first steps of school life seemed an eternity away and, in the best schoolboy fashion, one was able to identify oneself with such cowboy heroes as Bill Charles Starrett as *The Durango Kid*, Lash LaRue and Johnny Mack Brown. What a wealth of escapism was contributed to by those stars. It was with sadness, and an almost total disregard for my most intimate boyish feelings that I was to later learn through the written word that my hero, the tough, hard-hitting, fast-drawing but ageing and heavily built Johnny Mack Brown, when out of range of the camera lens, had to be lifted on and off his horse. How could they trifle with a schoolboy's affections with such assertions? But whether they were only celluloid heroes or not there is no doubting the impression they made on our young minds. After watching a *Lone Ranger* serial, we would come bursting out of the

Shack, galloping up Sandy Row, fervently smacking our backsides with one hand and with the other holding imaginary reins as we urged ourselves on to greater efforts singing as we went:

We are the mystery riders, the penny sliders, the hapney pokes.

Outside of my cowboy heroes my greatest idol was Buster Crabbe as Flash Gordon. It was my proud boast and no mean achievement in those days that I had never missed a serial. Imagine my frustration and annoyance when at the insistence of my mother, Peggy from next door, a young lady of my tender age, was to share with me the anticipated thrill of watching Flash about to explore the subterranean caverns under Ming's palace. I had hardly a fingernail left, biting through each one in turn the previous week as Flash and his companions escaped the dreaded clutches of the Stone Age men and were about to enter the mysterious caverns. And now the big moment for which I had waited all week had arrived and I didn't want the doubtful honour of sharing it with any hysterical female. But all seemed to go well. We laughed together through the Stoogies. We watched the spaceships leaving earth and settling on the forbidden planet and it was a signal to us that Flash was about to burst upon us in another action-packed adventure. The minutes passed, and Flash was well into the interior of the dreaded caves when out they came, totally unexpected in their suddenness. Even I couldn't control a nervous twitch as the clay men with their grotesque faces emerged from out of the clay walls of the caverns. But the reaction from my lady friend was equally sudden and just as uncontrollable, if not predictable, as she dived for cover behind the row of seats in front. The sobbing and crying from her rose and fell in its pitch, broken only intermittently by a sobbed plea for her domiciliary residence as she bawled out 'I wanna go home.' It appeared to come from the very depths of her being. How could I refuse such a request, so pathetically put, to take her home. As we started to leave, in the commotion, other patrons had become involved and were addressing me in no uncertain manner as to the desirability of escorting the young lady out of the cinema. Little passed between us as we made our way up Sandy Row towards home, stopping only now and then for me to implement an oft repeated threat of my father's and 'box her listener.'

One local church hall became a cinema for one night a week, opening its doors to us promptly at seven o'clock each Friday evening. And for the princely sum of a penny, provided under fourteen-year-olds with the opportunity to sit through such hair-raisers as *Who Killed Aunt Annie* or enjoy the tough antics of *New York's East Side Kids*. It was nicknamed the 'Penny Grope', a doubtful honour bestowed upon it from the youth of Sandy Row and beyond. It is with a sort of funny feeling of embarrassment that I now realize on reflection that I must, as the occasion warranted it, have unashamedly made my request for a penny for the Grope, completely unaware what the nickname meant to its older patrons.

The war in which my brother Davie was engaged 'over there' was to be brought much nearer home to us. Events in Europe had taken a more sinister twist as Hitler speedily brought his campaign in central Europe to a close, concentrating his war machine further afield in Russia and England. Soon the Luftwaffe was bombing the major cities in England. Next it was Belfast's and Sandy Row's turn, when a German bomb fell on the top end of Blythe Street, taking almost half of that end of the street with it and leaving a trail of death and destruction in its wake. I remember the first air raid on Belfast and Big Lil hastily fetching me out of bed, bringing me downstairs clad only in my combinations as the first incendiary bombs fell, lighting up the evening sky with a frightening glow. That evening we were on our own. I think my father was already fire-watching. The whole sky took on a reddish hue as the timber yards at the docks raged in a blazing inferno. I knew then, young and all as I was, that something new and terrible was happening to all of us. With this sudden twist of events, my father packed Big Lil and me and our newest arrival in the family, my baby brother Terry, off to the country. He remained behind in the city with extra duties, he was often employed as Supervisor in the morgue at the Belfast City Hospital during the worst nights of the air raids. And so at the tender age of eight, I bade farewell to Sandy Row, to my old haunts and familiar friends, to Jackie and my chums, and last of all to Miss Tate. It was well over two years before I was to make my return to my beloved Sandy Row.

Chapter 4
The Farmer's Boy

Once more my schooling was interrupted and during my
stay in the country became a thing of fits and starts with
large gaps in my attendance record. I am unable to recall
how I truly felt at my departure, probably I was so taken up
with a sense of adventure as to what lay ahead, or with the
feeling that anything would be better than my inglorious
beginnings at Workman School. Perhaps I was purposely
misinformed of the true nature and destination of our visit.
I can't honestly say that the country proved to be the best
thing that ever happened to me. I do not remember the
mode of travel to McKinstry's Hill any more than I could
describe the details of my birth. But there is no disputing
the fact that life precedes birth and in the chain of events
surrounding my life, Sandy Row preceded McKinstry's Hill.
Consequently like the experience of birth I had arrived into
a world of strange sights and sounds and my first reaction
was to kick up a rumpus.

The sudden change in my environment was too much for me to cope with, let alone the acceptance of a new school (I had just learnt to tolerate my previous one), especially when, before I had been able to settle in or see around me, I had the traumatic experience of witnessing Jean's daily departure for school. This, to say the least, left me rather subdued about school and indeed life in general. Jean was a young lady about a year older than me who, as a guest at the house where I was to live, had already been introduced to her new school. To watch her about to depart for school in the morning was a harrowing and frightening experience, even by my standards. Come school time she was physically escorted from the cottage, threatened, bullied, praised, extolled of the virtues of education, the terrible consequences of going through life stupid, and then threatened, bullied, praised etc. This love-hate relationship invoked by her departure usually continued on down the lane of the Hill until it was mercifully lost to the hearing. This to say the least had a profound influence on me, particularly with my past history; already I was planning that my stay at the new school would be a short one if Jean was any indication to go by. But having promised my mother to give my new school a fair chance and not allow myself to be unduly influenced by what I had seen of Jean (Jean having finally succumbed to the call of the city had left us), I arrived at my new school with the best intentions in the world.

I survived my initial entry and the morning passed uneventfully. We were allowed out about eleven o'clock for our morning break when something totally unpredictable occurred that was that was to put an intolerable strain on my most ardent resolutions. A big country boy named Jones singled me out during our playground activities and without waiting for any formal introductions began to put me through what I felt was some sort of question and answer exercise. 'What's your name and where do you come from?' As I was replying with the name 'Terry' he retorted, 'You're a townie aren't you?'[4]

To my amazement, he then burst out laughing. What was so funny about my baby brother to bring about such a reaction? I immediately began to feel very hostile to him as he towered over me. 'Terry,' he said, still laughing, 'Terry,' he repeated with great monotony, as if obsessed by the name. 'Terry, why that's a dog's name.' Now I had already developed strong and protective brotherly feelings for our new arrival and this sudden outburst was the proverbial last straw, whereupon I gave him a hefty and well-directed kick to the shins and, before he could recover, ran like the hammers straight out of the school and up the road, with his howls of pain and promises of retaliation spurring me on as I endeavoured to put as much mileage between me and this

---

[4] It is not known why Gordon used his brother's name in this exchange.

enraged country bumpkin as my overworked legs would allow. Halting only momentarily at the foot of the lane until I got my second wind, I didn't stop until I was well within the safety of our cottage. In retrospect, I suppose, although the circumstances were different there was a certain similarity between this and my first breach of school etiquette.

Two teachers accounted for the sum total of teaching staff, so my new school couldn't by any means be described as a sophisticated seat of high-powered learning. Yet neither was it a monolith of conveyor belt education, factory-produced, cold and impersonal. Miss Mairs was responsible for senior infants right through to third standard, while Mr Smylie accepted responsibility for the rest. One group was divided from the other by a partition wall which folded up concertina fashion as circumstances demanded, for instance during end of term parties or when the school had to be addressed as a whole. On first impressions the set up appealed to me as the ideal situation in which to find myself. Here I would be one among many lost in a sea of hopeless confusion; what a pleasant contrast it would be to the close supervision of Miss Tate, who I was firmly convinced was able to read my inmost thoughts. But as it so happened I had completely misread the situation, for in those demanding days of the war we were all urged unto greater efforts, bombarded as we were continually by the many pleas to raise our standards, whether it was in the garden or in the field of increased vigilance. Wherever we went we were reminded that our country required every man and woman 'to do his or her duty', and Miss Mairs was no exception, raising her standards par excellence. She travelled from Belfast by train to Moira where, at the railway station, she picked up the bicycle that helped her complete the few remaining miles to the school at Soldierstown. More than once, at the first snowflakes, I watched in hopeful anticipation that the weather would keep her away. But 'Through hail and high water', and always at the appointed time, she turned through the school gates pushing her bicycle. Like the poor referred to in the New Testament 'she was always with us'.

She was a very astute lady and, as I was to find, more than a match for all of us. As for close supervision, her motto was to 'divide and conquer'. Her instant reading sessions were a never-to-be-forgotten experience; she would suddenly leave off instructing one group and pounce upon another. On the instructions of 'Pens down!' we would be further informed to report to the front for reading, where half a dozen of us hastily gathered in front of her while she issued out readers to each of us. 'We are reading as you see from *The Wind in the Willows*, we shall begin with "Toad of Toad Hall.' We watched her attentively for the curt nod which was the signal for hostilities to begin. She lit from one to the other of us like a worker bee extracting nectar from some reluctant flower. Sometimes falling back on the same person twice or interrupting the reading in the middle of a sentence to catch the unwary. Woe betide the boy who lost his place, who fumbled when his turn came. Retribution was swift and painful. A well-bound and heavily backed copy of *The Wind in the Willows*, the personal property of Miss Mairs, directed to the side of the head was an effective way of making a point. Many a time, as a newcomer having difficulty following the local dialect, I was a recipient of the written word, but for Miss Mairs I have nothing but admiration. In our short acquaintance she did more for me than anyone, introducing me to a working knowledge of the three essentials.

After I had become familiar with the school and had time to take stock of my new surroundings I began to yearn immediately for my old home and the big city, and above all for Sandy Row and my old mates, for my old haunts around the tramway depot and up by the Jockey's, for pavements and streets and all the games associated with them. In an effort to console me, my father on his rare visits to us often praised the fresh air and healthy virtues of the country. I didn't always appreciate it when he would suddenly stop and instruct me to follow his example, as he came to attention inhaling and exhaling in-between pointed commendations on the benefits derived from a rural existence. I would have gladly swapped the sweet-scented smell of the hedgerows after rain for the Sandro's own peculiar aroma of sweaty bodies and black disinfectant swilled down by Robbie. In Sandy Row I felt secure surrounded by the tiny houses, row upon row of them, each one a legacy left to Belfast during the great industrial boom when the people flocked to the city in search of work. Here I felt lonely and insecure. There, even the trams thundering up our street first thing in the morning as they left the depot for their various destinations, and returning again last thing at night, gave me a feeling of belonging to a greater community outside our street – a sense of security and safety among the masses. Here I felt isolated, apart from the five cottages on our hill it seemed to me that there wasn't a dwelling place or soul to be found for miles. Everything appeared so vast and monotonous with nothing but fields and trees as far as the eye could see. I felt trapped and out of place with my surroundings; nostrils were invaded with new smells which I couldn't interpret like the aroma of fresh manure and decaying vegetation and country roads drenched in rain, of bulrushes and marshy ground, of silage and new-mown hay.

Then there were the tiny creatures which made life a nightmare for me; my revulsion of the snails which suddenly appeared at the base of the hedgerows after the rain, and my first experience on going to the spring well for water. Back home we didn't live in the Grand Central Hotel but at least on the turn of a tap we had running water. Here when we needed water we had to go down the lane from the Hill and across the lawn at Haze's Farm and descend the small stone steps which led to the well. Imagine my horror on disturbing the water with my pail to find that it was the home of frogs and other slimy creatures. Even the privacy of our loo was invaded by insects to which I had a particular aversion, these were earwigs, and we all knew the stories related in the city as to how these tiny insects got immense satisfaction from finding their way to a man's brain via his ear. Our loo was a dry toilet confined in a wooden sentry-like hut situated at the bottom of our garden. These tiny creatures scurried in and out of the spaces in the woodwork. From a sitting position I was alarmed to discover that they had even occupied the inside of the roof. I sat in fear of them dropping onto my head. For some time to come, going to the loo proved a difficult exercise for me. My antics lending a certain similarity to the remedy for hiccups I once read put forward by a doctor, in which he advocated the drinking of a glass of water with the fingers stuck in the ears.

It was, therefore, no spontaneous acceptance of my new life on my part, but rather an uphill adjustment in which the country had to fight hard in her efforts to win me over. I think she almost succeeded, but this was mostly due to the friendship extended to me by Teddy Dugan. He it was who revealed his most intimate secrets to me. I was filled with complete admiration for him. Though only a few years older than me, he seemed in everything relating to the country the true professional. Because of the labour shortage on the land at that time I had even known the farmer to call at our school requesting his services, such was his skill and all-round ability. He became my teacher and I his willing pupil;

through him the trees yielded their names to me and from him I learnt the best kindling wood for the fire. No tree was too tall to climb or nest too perilously high to yield up its secrets to us, no bird too difficult to identify.

The mystery of seed time and harvest took on a whole new meaning for me and no task about the farm too menial for me to undertake. I spent hours perched on the tractor, sitting behind the farmer while the seed was sown and the fields rolled in preparation for an abundant harvest of wheat and corn (the merest whiff of diesel fumes never fails to activate nostalgic memories of those happy carefree days). Then quite often in the evening Teddy would bring me with him as he accompanied the farmer in his car to pastures many miles distant from the farm. On arrival we would cross the fields and check the cattle against the tally given to us by the farmer. It was great fun trying to persuade the cattle to stay in one place while all this was happening. All the while, with no great sense of urgency, the Lagan Canal flowed past the back of our cottages, twisting and turning on its appointed course to Lough Neagh. It was always a great thrill when I was permitted to go with our next door neighbour along its banks on one of his illicit fishing trips. before the advent of darkness we often made our way through the forest that lined the bank of the canal, the air heavy with the scent of pine wood, choosing our steps carefully when we crossed a stretch of woodland where the undergrowth rose and fell in sharp ridges on its perpetual slope to the canal.

Many a startled rabbit we raised as the woods echoed to the sound of the wood pigeon intent on making our presence known throughout the forest. But we pushed on undeterred, until, our objective reached, we laid out our long lines, each one carefully hidden for the night. Our mission accomplished we returned in hopeful anticipation that some hungry pike might rise to our bait. Like someone who has just been given a privileged glimpse into the past I had often stood on the banks of the canal watching the men from the Hill using fishing methods which must have dated from time immemorial. As with great expertise they waded out from the bank and among the bulrushes literally spearing the perch and eels with the sharp teeth of their rakes. Upon the Hill the resulting catch was placed in buckets of water and hung on the branches of a suitable tree. The canal also gave Teddy and me many hours of peaceful relaxation. From the back of our cottage we would race down the hill eagerly seeking possession of the flat-bottomed punt usually tied at the canal's edge at a point in direct line with the rear of our cottage. With a push and a heave on the oars we would send her gliding far out into the mainstream of the river. From this vantage point we watched the swans nesting and guarding their precious brood deep in the long bulrushes until our attention was further taken up with the submarine antics of the water hen as we startled her and she submerged to pop up yards away. This always fascinated us as we tried to guess the next spot on the river where she was likely to emerge. With flat stones previously collected we tested our skill from the boat by skimming the smooth stones across the surface of the canal in an effort to reach the far bank. It was amazing with a little practice and a really flat stone the distance that could be achieved before the stone finally sank.

Mr Jolly, who worked as a labourer on Haze's Farm and lived in the cottage beside us, took a keen interest in the young lad from the city. Soon, as a result of his patience and advice, I was able to turn our back garden into a veritable vegetable plot yielding vegetables of every shape and size, from beans to beetroot. It was my pride and joy and the admiration of the different visitors we had from town and, I believe, influential in helping me to be so readily accepted by my new-found friends from the Hill. It was always with a feeling of pride and a sense of achievement that this tenderfoot was able to stand apparently identified with his country cousins as they mocked the evacuees from the city, calling them townies. How I had once hated that name. Now I had passed my initiation rites I had been accepted. I was a man of the soil 'of the earth, earthy'.[5] Not only did my knowledge and awareness of the country increase but my physique also. I became stronger, more daring and more confident of my own ability to pursue an end through to its successful conclusion. As I did, I am afraid I also became

---

[5] 1 Corinthians 15:47.

arrogant and more aloof with my friends from the city in relation to country matters. I was reluctant to share my secrets with them. After all, my new-found knowledge had not been easily come by. But all the while my friendship and admiration for Teddy deepened.

Teddy had four sisters, Peggy, Florence, Lilian and Joan. It was Lilian, (who was the same age as myself) who had been the most critical of me during my tenderfoot days. It was her more than even Teddy who regarded the townies with a great deal of scorn and ridicule, and it was her acceptance of me that I valued more than anything. About this time Lilian's oldest sister had gone off to the big city to work, of all places, in the district of my old haunts in Sandy Row, in the Le Tastie, a meat shop specializing in meat pies and not a stone's throw away from No. 12. Seeing her start off for work always brought on an intense yearning for absent friends, so much so that I decided secretly to lie in wait for her return, anxious to see if in some mystical way I had communicated something of my personality through her which might find a response as she traversed so near to my old haunts. Perhaps she would even see Jackie at play and some strange force of unconscious communication would flow from one to the other making itself known to me on her return. Alas she returned the vehicle of no projected thought processes and with certainly no telepathic message for me. Rather dejected, I watched her pass. From this young country girl, glad to be home after her long day of toil and travel, there wasn't even the slightest hint of any association with my old existence. It was not what I had hoped for but, consoling myself, I settled down in the spot behind the hedge from where I had scrutinized her approach to the Hill. I began to bridge the distance between Soldierstown and the Row by the quickest and cheapest form of travel still in existence as I prepared to dream myself back into the Row and into the pie shop where I was completely surrounded by luscious, hot, sweet-smelling pies all begging to be ravaged.

I had a real live link with No. 12. This came through my father on those weekends when he was free to visit us. I would leave McKinstry's Hill with plenty of time to spare as I set out to meet my father, taking the Duggan's roughhaired fox terrier with me. With a true canine affection for my father, he was always as excited about the whole thing as I was, having at one time persisted in following him some miles to the railway station on his return home, and where he was only restrained from entering the railway carriage with the help of a railway official. It must be admitted, however, that my interest wasn't wholly filial and not entirely uninfluenced by the candy apples I knew he would be carrying, bought on his way to the railway station at the wee homemade-sweet shop on Hope Street, Sandy Row. We usually met him halfway at the stone bridge spanning the canal.

On the far side of the river from our house and at its widest point was one of my favourite retreats. It was a high sloping field stretching right down to the edge of the tow-path in a huge blanket of pale yellow, being literally covered with large clusters of wild primroses. Needless to say it was known to us as primrose hill. Often I would go there and sit in deep reflection – it was the ideal setting as I pondered on the new life unfolding in front of me. Even after the last primrose had faded it always held for me that certain feeling of other worldliness and old world charm. Perhaps because it was from here that I could sit and watch the Lagan Canal, flanked on the far side at its bend by the forest in which I had spent so many happy hours, ebb its way slowly past the fields at the back of our cottages. It almost seemed at one with the character of the people of those parts, steady and sure with little undercurrents of strongly held convictions. From here I could also see the backs of our cottages distinct against the outline of the sky huddled together as if in united defiance against the elements. Further down the river I could just about make out the little sandy inlet tucked-underneath the bank and over which the forest towered at its thickest part. It was here that we had come upon the carcass of Sandy the dog, washed up on this tiny inshore.

Sandy was part whippet and part, I suppose, anyone's guess, but as youngsters he had won the lasting admiration of us all. His speed of movement and jumping ability, together with his natural friendliness, left us spellbound and endeared him to everyone. One evening in the middle of winter, when the ice covering the canal was at its thickest, an overzealous and reckless Sandy, despite our cries of alarm, bounded across the ice in pursuit of some swans that had made a small pond for themselves in the middle of the canal, at the weakest part of the ice. Ignoring our frantic appeals for him to return, he blundered on, slipping and sliding as the ice stripped him of his agility and dignity, reducing him to a pathetic creature spurred on by some blind instinct from his distant past. The swans, as if in answer, spread their mighty wings with a gracefulness and mobility which only highlighted and mocked the hopelessness of Sandy's predicament. Soon they were airborne and poor Sandy was left to act out this senseless tragedy on his own, trapped in the pond so recently vacated by the swans, surrounded by a river of unyielding ice. As a small boy standing on the bank of the canal, helpless to do anything, it was my first introduction to pain and suffering, and my first lesson in our own inadequacy. His strange animal entreaties went unanswered, except for the pitiful echoes that tore at the stunned silence which had enveloped us – it was an eerie feeling, but at least in some vicarious way it was an experience which I shared with him as I watched him disappear beneath the ice. And even the river, cold and indifferent at the first hint of spring, paid her own belated tribute and yielded up his last remains for burial.

The real atmosphere of the country comes across during the long winter evenings; it is a mood missed by the casual visitor and lost on the sceptic. With the honeymoon period of summer over it is in the winter that the country bares her soul. On a winter's evening we sat in our cottage, gathered around the log fire and thinking profound thoughts concerning our environment, as primitive man must have done as he was confronted by the forces of nature, over which he had no control and under which he felt so helpless. Unable to leave the cottage, we would discuss with the ready enthusiasm of small boys the thunder and the lightning. Our cottage having a tin roof, we knew full well the experience of the lightning flash and its final explosion on impact as it crashed upon our roof, but of the thunder in the sky, we were not so sure; was it really God rearranging his furniture in Heaven or was it God speaking in no uncertain manner to the Devil? Was the banshee, as was said, an old woman and was her moaning wail the forerunner of a death? And what lethal and sinister power surrounded the hawthorn if brought into the house in full bloom? Did the spirits of the dead haunt the old graveyard just beyond the Hill? Were the dogs afraid to go there once the early winter's darkness settled over the Hill? Such rural and varied philosophical thoughts helped relieve the boredom of many a long and lonely winter's evening. But the winter evenings were a part of the country I never fully accepted, so my conversion was anything but complete. I guess I was not seasoned enough or tough enough. I expected too much and gave too little in return. Our relationship had not been 'for better or for worse'. I suppose even in our highest moments I was still conscious of a sense of loneliness and isolation, mainly at night and always in winter. It was then, I believe, that the country lost out in the struggle to win over my soul.

One winter's evening as one of my nightly duties I made my way down the lane to the lawns on Haze's Farm where, from under the giant beech trees surrounding the entrance to the farm, I gathered the kindling wood from the many branches blown down by the storm. This huge lawn had given birth to its own special brand of shared memories involving the redoubtable Teddy and me. Brought along by Teddy it was from here that I had stood captivated as the farmer removed the last obstinate tree stumps with a charge of gelignite blowing them to kingdom come. It was on this same lawn that I watched the farmer raise his shotgun, sending the poor wood pigeon hurtling through the trees as, seriously wounded, it gradually lost elevation, while Teddy and I raced after it as we followed its hapless flight into a large sycamore where we almost lost it in a cloud of feathers as it crashed into branch after branch on its way to the ground, now no longer a thing of beauty but a gory mess of blood and feathers. As I gathered my wood, as if seeking a necessary safety valve, my thoughts would turn to happier times such as when, with cries of delight, we gathered the ripe walnuts from the vast walnut tree growing on the lawn over to the right of the little path which led to the farm. Under its spreading branches we stuffed our jerseys full of those delicious nuts, still clad in their green jackets. Our hands and clothing covered with the yellow dye which simply oozed from the covering of green around the walnuts. Our harvest gathered, we looked as if we had been immersed in iodine, but this little peculiarity we regarded as secondary to the scrumptious feast that was the happy outcome of our labours. Teddy said I had once camped on this same lawn when we had to make a speedy withdrawal from the orchard, but not before we had to contend with a barbed wire fence as we made our escape. In our haste I received a six inch gash on my thigh from which the blood simply poured, but on we fled having drawn upon ourselves the attention of the irate farmer. The scar which it left I regarded as a souvenir that served to remind me of those exciting days. That evening as I began the job of tying into bundles the different piles of wood I had collected I felt more than satisfied with my efforts for I had come to regard myself as something of an old hand. After all it was over two years since I had left the big smoke behind.

Suddenly as if in bitter contrast to the warm reminiscences of summer the winter's solitude gave way to the ghostly shrill of a train homeward-bound. It was a sickening sound as over the night air and across the fields and hills the taunting message came mocking me in my loneliness. It left me with a numbed and empty feeling as in my thoughts I followed her back to the back streets from whence she came and to where I belonged – as if some greater part of me must forever respond when she beckoned. I was homesick and I hated it, and this made me angry with myself, angry with Hitler, angry with the war, angry with anything or anyone who had shared in any way any responsibility for my being there. The warm recollections of summer had indeed changed into the cold sobriety of winter. For with a greater sense of discontent and dissatisfaction I once more gazed across the lawn. The friendly farm looked almost bleak and inhospitable in its winter setting. And from there my gaze wandered to the well, its approach barred by a sea of squelching mud. Close by stood the walnut tree; ravaged by winter it looked naked and barren, the merest gesture of its former self. Across the far side of the lawn, encircling the orchard, stretched the barbed wire fence, its sharp teeth more menacing than ever as they cringed in protest at the wind's casual disregard for their ability to deter. From the barbed wire fence, as if following a natural and logical association of ideas, my gaze turned in on myself and to the scar on my leg. Once my pride and joy, it now looked an ugly thing in its winter hue of blue and purple, a senseless violation of my young flesh.

The moment of truth had come, and it was useless to pretend any longer. I had been no more willing to conform or adjust than I was to accept or identify myself with the singing during those early days at Soldierstown School. We often sang 'The Minstrel Boy' and 'Little Brown Jug', but when 'The Farmer's Boy' was sung, with its usual enthusiasm, my city heart rebelled. For as we sang I would take stock of my classmates and come to the conclusion that it was right and proper for them to sing this country boy's anthem, whereas I felt in some strange way, which I couldn't explain, that for me to take part in the singing was to accept the inevitable. To sing the words was to be bound by them, like some passionate supplication requesting the Almighty to plan out our lives in an agricultural setting.

To reap and sow
To plough and mow
To be a Farmer's Boy.

Not for this boy. I was son to a father who was a convinced town dweller; the streets and pavements were my parish. So when the time came for one to leave in that Spring of 1944 I must confess I was a willing participant to whatever set of events or circumstances had made my parents decide to take me home again to the big smoke. I left with fond memories of McKinstry's Hill and the Lagan Valley and a treasured experience of a part of life which I wouldn't have missed for the world, the value of which, both physically and spiritually, was to stand by me in the years to come.

Thirty-three years later I returned to McKinstry's Hill for the first time since I left all those years ago, prompted by doubts which the passage of time had given birth to. Was it something in my past which I had greatly exaggerated or even completely distorted? Had my memory played tricks on me or was it a creation of some wish fulfilment that my urban existence had yearned for but been denied? On that beautiful summer afternoon as I left Moira Station with the homing instinct of a prize racing pigeon, I was conscious of treading ground which had been a real and important part of my childhood. Proceeding down the road from the railway station I instinctively turned left in anticipation of the tavern I expected to find. When we sang in school 'There's a Tavern in the Town' I always associated the original tavern in the song with the beautiful old country tavern close by the corner where the two roads met. Sure enough there it stood, a very smart extension had been added to it, but there was still enough of the old tavern left to catch a glimpse of its charm and elegance. I continued on up the road past the tavern of my song until I came to the little village of Soldierstown. Turning left I started to climb the hill, hesitating only to glance to the right and up the road whose apex reached the skyline at a place known to us as rabbit hill, so called because of the numerous burrows which could be seen at its top. On reaching the summit I could see clearly the farm on the right of the road where if my memory serves me well, lived two boys of my own age who attended our school and under whose sandy hair were the largest freckles I had ever seen. Further on and to the right lay Jordan's Farm. Almost before I realized it I had arrived at the stone bridge spanning the canal where I had often met my father. From the Lagan towpath I entered the field known to us as primrose hill. The primroses had long given of their best, but there was ample evidence of better days, seen in the luscious green foliage that still remained. Looking across the Lagan I could see the cottages just as I had known them, adorning the hill like silent witnesses to man's faith in the consistency of nature.

On the bend of the canal I could see once more the tiny inlet upon which the river had given back to us the dead body of Sandy. I turned back up the towpath onto the bridge. Once on the road again I kept on walking past the lane leading to the hill, past the lawn on the left and the little path to the well. Soon I was looking in through the railings at my old school.

Thirty years is a long time, but I had been assured I had seen and felt enough. These were no fantasy dreams, but stored memories come alive as out of the past they came like ghosts of forgotten actions. Leaving my old school I headed back past the church and the graveyard, noticing as I did the figure bent over a grave, his face hid from me. In obedience to some inner impulse telling me to wait I halted and watched the lone figure tending the grave. Suddenly he was conscious of my observations and said 'Good afternoon' with the courtesy common in such parts, but at the same time no doubt wondering who this stranger was. 'Good afternoon, you're Mr Wilson aren't you?' (Mr Wilson belonged to our little community on the Hill.) His reply in the affirmative clothed my last ghost in flesh and blood. I turned away, continuing on down the road humming to myself as I went, 'The Farmer's Boy', stopping for a moment along the hedgerow to pick a 'Devil's Eye'.

Soldierstown School, 1940

Chapter 5

A Welcome Return to The Row

Sandy Row in comparison to the country affected me like a welcome breath of fresh air. This odd claim is probably better understood from the following analogy concerning my father who first thing on rising for work grabbed out in desperation for a Woodbine cigarette, which he immediately shoved in his mouth. Though a very articulate person, what proceeded forth after this usually amounted to a garbled approbation to the Almighty for its soothing and healing virtues during which he proceeded to cough his head off.

Nevertheless my nose told me I had arrived and what more fitting arrival for a loyal son than via the Boyne Bridge. From here the first aroma that I renewed acquaintance with came from Murray's Tobacco Factory; it was a smell that I always associated with my eager trips over the Boyne Bridge on my way to the Coliseum. And of course there was the acquired smell of the drum-maker's shop. Further up the Row I encountered those smells which I had at one time given up all hope of ever experiencing again. The working man's treat of freshly cooked pigs feet attractively laid out in small pyramids in the shop windows and of course the smell of hot fish and chips freshly dressed with salt and vinegar, while the mixture of mothballs and second-hand clothing was a clear indication that I was on the same side as Maggie Moore's. On the other side of the road in a sort of halfway house position stood the Old House at Home where the wooden porter barrels arranged outside like sentinels in the street lent their own unique contribution to the overall smell, and at the same time served as a constant reminder (if any was needed) of the refreshments offered within. But reserved for the true connoisseur at the top end of Sandy Row (that end which housed the local Orange Hall and which for me made it the best end, and the end where I lived) was the Blacksmith's shop at the corner of Moore's Place on the Donegal Road and opposite Primitive Street Methodist Church.

It was seldom, if ever, that the Blacksmith's shop failed to delay my return from school. I would stand for long periods gazing into its interior, drinking in the atmosphere and allowing my nostrils the treat of identifying the various smells of hot charcoal and coke with that of nervous horse flesh and the never to be forgotten aroma released in a puff of blue and yellow smoke during the act of shoeing, as red hot iron and hoof fused in one. I never visited the place without thinking of my Uncle Joe. If the stories that the blacksmith told me were anything to go by he was quite a character about the Row and further afield because of his involvement with horses, both as a pleasure and a profession. He was known locally as Horsey Freeman. He worked with them and earned his living by them down in the great markets of our city. Eventually his love for horses followed him into the Great War as is borne out by the photograph we have of him in the uniform of the 8th Hussars (also nicknamed the cherry pickers) complete with pillbox hat, riding boots and whip.

I had arrived back into my old haunts in time for the marriage of the May Queen, this was a ceremony duly acted out each year in districts all over Belfast. The dress for the Queen was made out of coloured paper while a suitable headdress was devised out of a piece of old net curtain. All that was required to create the traditional suitor was a little soot. The only props needed were provided by a long pole (suitably decorated with coloured pieces of string and paper), each end of which was supported by members of her entourage, with the Queen and Darkie[6] taking their places in between and grasping the pole from behind. The principal participants in this little, travelling street show were the

---

[6] The book *Boys and Girls Come Out to Play* by Maurice Leyden, contains a collection of Irish Singing Games. On page 100 and 101 it states that at the beginning of the last century, Mayday was a holiday for chimney sweeps. They were a colourful sight parading through the streets. During the 1800s, it was normal practice to use young children for cleaning chimneys and inevitably their faces were blackened with soot for the Mayday celebrations. This explains why these songs have reference to "the darkie'".

Queen and the Darkie who had avowed his love for her to the point of asking her hand in marriage. This was announced to all and sundry with the singing of the verse 'The Darkie said he'd marry her, marry her, marry her'. As a Darkie it was not the first time I had lost my heart to a willing May Queen. The versatility of the Queen was much in evidence by the fact that we danced along singing: 'Our Queen can burl her leg, burl her leg, burl her leg,' with the corresponding response from her Majesty. Any good Darkie worth his salt never allowed himself to be outdone by this with a smart tumble over the pole. All the while the little play enacted itself we came in periodically singing 'Our Queen's up the river and we'll keep her up for ever with a Ya, Ya, Ya, Ya, Ya.' Next the qualities of the Queen as a marriage candidate were further proclaimed as we sang 'Our Queen can ate a hard bap, ate a hard bap, ate a hard bap.' This latest virtue of the May Queen always puzzled me as a boy. I could never decide whether eating a hard bap was regarded as a feat in itself or the Queen's declared willingness to conform should the couple fall on hard times. Still it was all great fun and at the same time provided a certain remunerative income for us as we danced along and rattled our tin can.

One thing my return to the Row proved was that I was completely out of touch. For one thing our play areas about the streets were to a certain extent restricted. Air-raid shelters and static water tanks had mushroomed all over our district. But as events were to prove, it was not only the street scenes with which I was completely out of touch. This was brought home to me under rather painful circumstances. On one Sabbath morning Jackie and I (of with whom I had renewed my acquaintance and discovered to my horror that back to back he had at least two inches advantage over me) set off dressed in our Sunday best. I can't imagine now what the attraction was, but we had stopped at the Claremont shop and soon our faces were pressed against the window when along came this other lad and roughly pulled Jackie away from the window, declaring in the same instant that maybe now he could get a better look. I was amazed to discover that Jackie seemed to accept this almost as a normal course of events, which in itself should have been a warning to me. But my first reaction was an instinctive one for me, for I had foolishly acquired the unreliable and sometimes dangerous habit of measuring human potential in feet and inches and I noted right that this other lad was, if anything, smaller than me. Rather brashly I enquired 'You aren't going to let him get away with that are you?' In reply Jackie winced and managed to look like someone who is about to witness an unhappy and probably unnecessary accident. Quickly the course of events switched and I became the centre of attention as this unwelcome intruder moved closer to me and posed the following curt and highly emotive question, punctuating each word as he did so with a sharp prod of his finger into my chest. 'And what are you going to do about it?'

What followed was inevitable. Soon we were milling about the pavement. From a close quarter exchange I stepped back, blood pouring from my nose. This enraged me and I immediately renewed our exchanges. whereupon a lady, who had just completed her Sunday morning devotions, decided to intervene in this unseemly bout of fisticuffs, first by a spirited appeal to our better natures and then with her umbrella. As she flayed about her with her brolly, she shouted of the terrible fate awaiting those who would deign to desecrate the Sabbath in this manner. When she had eventually parted us this guardian of the Lord's day noticed my blouse covered in blood and immediately decided that I had been involved more in the role of receiver than aggressor and promptly produced a penny which she deposited in the pocket of my blouse. This event, happening, as it did, early in my return to the big smoke, was to prove a pointer in the course that my life was to take. As we left the scene Jackie hastened to point out to me that in my ignorance I had taken on the local hard chaw.

Yes, I suppose I could claim to have been out of touch. In spite of this I was to return to Workman School in a blaze of glory, but I had to be accepted first. This meant that as a newcomer I had to prove myself. The trouble sprang from the fact that Miss Mairs had done her work so well. Indeed

I was often embarrassed by the attentions of Miss Watchhorn my new teacher. She would bring me up to the front of the class and point me out to all as a shining example, a prodigal returned and capable of the most tremendous mental gymnastics. Then she would get me to go through the sums on the blackboard at great speed, after which I was hugged, squeezed, given money and sent home early; really it was all too much! And too much it was for some who had to suffer on in silence. Soon my pencil went missing, next a rubber. I saw it as a direct challenge to my masculinity. Needless to say the culprit and I retired to a nearby entry after school, only this time it was I who had a bloody nose at the other end of my fist.

After this life at Workman School found its own level for me and, apart from further honours thrust upon me like ringing the school bell, I found myself surprisingly capable of settling down and enjoying my new found popularity. In school we were all conscious of our involvement in the war situation. This was due to the efforts the school authorities asked us to put into such campaigns as gathering waste paper and collecting Savings Bonds. I even remember purchasing a savings stamp down at the 'Blitzed Square' in High Street and sticking it onto a huge bomb which we were told was destined for Nazi Germany.

As youngsters we had already felt the pinch of the war for sweets were rationed and you simply couldn't get fireworks anywhere. At Halloween we had to improvise with such things as syrup tins into which we put carbine, lit it, replaced the lid and retired; the resulting explosion could be quite frightening. The blackout we accepted as inevitable as a counter measure against the Nazi bombers. Along with the blackout, black bread, margarine, saccharine, powdered eggs and painted legs became a way of life.

Into this little kingdom of wartime restrictions came the American, straight from the land of plenty. These brash, whiskey-drinking, gum- chewing extroverts had left behind their oil wells and ranches while they sorted out the war game, or so they told us. And in doing so they unintentionally created a lot of discontent with their existence from a certain section of our community who, it may be said, unashamedly sought their favours.

Quite often during the summer I availed myself of a popular pastime for a Sunday afternoon by taking a tram ride to the terminus where, on the outskirts of Belfast, I explored such places as Greencastle, Ligoniel, Bellevue and the Ballygomartin and Whiterock areas. On these occasions I was usually accompanied by my young brother who was now almost three years old. More often than not we were stopped by these Americans and my brother became the object of their attention. They were simply intrigued by the colour of his pure blonde hair and showed their admiration in typical American fashion by giving us gum and sometimes money. But my most lasting impression of them came from the

Company billeted at the Methodist Church Hall in Fountainville Avenue. We would hang around their billet and attempt, by our keen sense of smell, to snare in some way the gastronomical delights which we believed were taking place within. Sometimes we were rewarded, but one poor misguided lad, whom I recognized as coming from the Row, had apparently decided, when the opportunity arose, to sample uninvited some of those tasty American dishes. I will always remember his pathetic look of apprehension and fear as, caught in the act, his pleas ignored, he was marched off by this big American. For a long time I wondered what fate had befallen him and if society had given him another chance. I never returned there again, though not from any sense of fear, but rather from a strong feeling of identification with his obvious plight.

Whether we liked the American or not we couldn't ignore his impact on our lives: his introduction of new sounds into our current vocabulary, words like doughboys, jeeps, Lucky Strike, candies and of course the mighty dollar, and other items from the rubber industry which have never lost their popularity or potency since.

As a young boy I was prejudiced against these strange soldiers who seemed to slouch along our city streets wearing their chevrons upside down. The British Tommy was my hero and for me the ideal of what a fighting soldier should look like, but now that I am older and more mature I must express my gratitude to those lads from across the continent who came to see the war in Europe in a worldwide context. In this we shared a common identity.

Most boys, we are told, want to be an engine driver when they grow up, but I feel that few boys ever see themselves as grown up; instead they live in the present, with no ending. My imagination shifted in a duel-like contest between being a legionnaire and a sailor. It was usually after reading such books as P. C. Wren's *Wages of Virtue* and his *Beau* series or those like *I wear the Burnous*, a thrilling account of a legionnaire's many adventures among the Arabs, that I saw myself as a legionnaire. All that I required to help fulfil this ambition was my skullcap under which I had tucked my handkerchief so that it hung down at the back to shelter my neck from the lethal rays of the intense Sahara sun. My black gaberdine raincoat buttoned at the neck and hanging over my shoulders served adequately as a cloak to protect me from the cold night air of the desert. As a potential sailor I read and reread such novels as *Midshipman Easy* and the *Hornblower* series by C. S. Forester. Indeed I was the proud possessor of a seaman's manual, which I devoutly pored over, learning by heart such things as semaphore and Morse code, and the names and locations of the various stations aboard ship, until I came to regard myself as something of an old sea dog in such matters.

When I went to Ma Carroll's (the wee tobacconist's shop at our street corner) on an errand I was never left in any doubt as to my true calling in life; the sea won every time.

The predominant odour of the shop came from snuff, so heavy did it hang in the air that one's sinuses immediately responded on entering. Sweets and snuff alike found their way over the counter, poured into home-made newspaper pokes from the deft but somewhat shaky hand of Ma Carroll. Snuff may have been the prime smell of the shop but the all-pervading atmosphere smacked of the tang of the sea. Once inside the shop I generally expected to meet, instead of Ma Carroll shuffling out in answer to the elaborate bell mechanism that signalled one's arrival in the shop, some of the more dubious old salts from the *Admiral Benbow*. The centre of the shop was given over to a large advertisement showing Drake engaged in his final game of bowls prior to defeating the Spanish Armada. In the window hung a print of a famous scene depicting the *Mayflower* leaving Plymouth on its journey to the Americas. Another picture displayed on the counter showed a seafaring gentleman pointing out sailing ships at anchor in the bay to some children on the quayside. All around the shop were large displays of Player's cigarette cards portraying the bearded head of a sailor enclosed in a lifebelt, on the background of which were ships of the line. It was easy, after soaking up the atmosphere of Ma Carroll's, to leave the shop clutching the jackknife my brother Davie had given me on his last leave and, in a flight of fancy transport myself to some far distant part of the Caribbean. But as I always imagined myself as a legionnaire or a sailor in a wartime situation, events looming on the horizon in the shape of VE Day were to lessen the pressure of either calling on me, and soon I was to settle for a more land-based activity.

At the impressionable old age of eleven, and having exhausted all that Workman School was permitted to impart in the way of education, I was compelled to move on. Even though Linfield School, known locally as the Big School, catered for the Sandy Row area I was to pursue my education at Fane Street Primary. Situated in a somewhat middle-class area, its setting brought home to me for the first time an awareness that I belonged to a working-class district. At that time no more than half a dozen of us attending the school came from Sandy Row and consequently we journeyed there as a small group. Once, as we returned home, a number of pupils who resided in that area shouted out to us as we passed, 'There go the boys from the back streets.' We had of course an answer for that one. Nevertheless it left a deep and lasting impression upon me. The back streets? Sandy Row, the back streets? But with VE day already on us there was no other place I'd sooner come from, no other area I'd sooner be than in and from the back streets.

Only they could have put on such a patriotic show of loyalty and uninhibited enthusiasm for the end of the war. We celebrated it in true Sandy Row fashion. Everything, and I mean everything – lamp posts, pavements, kerb stones and gable walls – was painted red, white and blue. It had been said that anyone remaining stationary for any length of time ran the risk of being painted into the decor. Bunting criss-crossed the streets and street parties and impromptu concerts were the order of the day. Gramophones blared out such songs as 'Clementine' and 'South of the Border' along with other renderings less conventional and more related to our tribal differences, but who cared? We were celebrating in the best way we knew how. The highlight of the celebrations and my most lasting memory of VE Day came with the parade down to the City Hall. Never have I seen so many people of all denominations before, or indeed since, gathered in one place, of one attitude of mind, so less self-conscious and so determined in their aspirations for peace. Adults and children alike we dressed up for the parade. Still fresh in my memory is a picture of one lady dressed up as Carmen Miranda. How she danced and sang. To me she was symbolic of the overall spirit of the celebrations entered into so unreservedly and spontaneously by the people. We were witnessing the release of tensions and fears that had been bottled up for years. It was as if we had captured the spirit and atmosphere of the Mardi Gras, as in a carnival mood we paraded down Sandy Row. We were recording a brief moment of history in which we were getting a glimpse of the people of Sandy Row and beyond at their best. The true spirit of Ulster was never far from the surface and this was an opportunity for Ulster to fully express itself; it was Ulster 'letting her hair down'. It was a moment I was proud to have been able to share with her.

Chapter 6

The Bonfire and the Glorious Twelfth

The big annual event in our lives, of course, was the Twelfth of July and the night preceding it. In our district to be permitted to collect the wood for the bonfire was taken as a graduation into the circle of an older group of boys whose ages ranged from eleven to fourteen. My final acceptance into this group came with a tremendous feeling of elation when I was included in those detailed to meet at our entry in the early hours of the morning. That particular morning we met as arranged with ropes tied around our waists and equipped with axes, well-prepared for the forage for wood that would take us into the depths of the Black Forest that lined the flank of the River Lagan at Stranmillis and Malone. On our return our first detail consisted of seeing that the wood was safely stored in the entry used by us for this purpose, but even then our task was only partially completed. With the existence of a keen sense of rivalry among the streets in the Row for whoever had the largest bonfire, it was not unknown for one street to make a raid upon the wood of another. It was with this ever-present threat in mind that we immediately posted guards on our wood with special reference to Hunter Street, who we saw as our immediate rivals and whom we knew from past experience were quite capable of pinching it.

The Hunter Street area was always regarded by us as the tight end, in it we believed resided the heaviest concentration of local strong-arm men in the whole of Sandy Row. From this area it was possible to hire bicycles by the hour and handcarts of every shape and size for every conceivable purpose, from selling sticks or fruit to moving furniture. Most of the local barrow boys who plied their wares about the Row and up and around the residential areas of Stranmillis and Malone resided there. Coming as we did from the tramway area it was seldom, if ever, that we ventured into it on our own, and then only out of necessity. Alas the visit of a favourite uncle of mine (who was of all things a school board member by profession) was to bring about this rare solo excursion into enemy territory, with an outcome which, to say the least, was rather embarrassing.[7] The chat in No. 12 was good, the subject as predictable as ever, about old times. My uncle always had a

---

[7] The favourite uncle was Francis Charters Skelly the 'beaky man'. He was actually Gordon's older cousin, Francis was born Gordon Victor Skelly and his name was changed at 3 months of age. Gordon was called after him Gordon Victor Skelly Freeman.

hearty laugh with my father when they discussed shared experiences from out of the past. A favourite comment of his was to compare the old days in their house (my uncle was reared by my father's mother) with being as good, indeed better, than the Palladium. They had well-warmed to their favourite topic when my uncle suggested that as a special treat I should go for some ice cream sliders to a shop in the City Street area. The evening was late and it was blackout, of course, as I left our house equipped with the necessary money and a plate. I arrived at the shop having made a successful detour around hostile territory by travelling the main thoroughfare of Sandy Row. Standing at the door of the shop with the purchased sliders my confidence returned and, so eager to get to grips with my promised slider with the minimum of delay, I decided on a shortcut. My route would be along Britannic Street and Felt Street and down Hunter Street then across the Donegal Road, through the wee entry and home. But the plate was over large and heavy (one of Big Lil's best), the sliders piled high, and I was soon tired. In consequence I held the plate with both hands, unable even to muster an occasional lick, stretching my arms to their full extent in order to ease the tension on them. I must admit that my posture must at times have resembled that of someone making an offering to the gods. Others lurking in the darkness must have been similarly impressed for almost as if by magic in the inky blackness my sliders disappeared. It was accomplished in the most professional manner and was entirely painless. I didn't even feel a thing. Rather bewildered I made for the nearest available source of light where all that I perceived was an empty plate. Tangible evidence that they hadn't fallen foul of some mysterious spirit of the night was left by the delicate criss-crossed pattern that now decorated Big Lil's plate, created, no doubt, by grubby fingers and from an intense desire on the part of their owners to partake.

On the evening of the eleventh, prior to lighting the bonfire, we always had a party. It was strictly confined to those who had taken part in the gathering of the wood. This party was usually financed by collections made during the period when the wood was gathered. That night we retired late, grubby and dirty but with a keen sense of accomplishment. We had all played our part, we had watched over our bonfire and seen it grow and were satisfied with the end result. The following day it was up to the Orangemen as they made their traditional walk to the field.

Looking back on those early days, I can now say, grubby and dirty we may have been, but such was our keen sense of involvement that never once, as the celebrations drew to a close, did I have any reason to feel morally unclean. Neither was I aware of having directed my feelings or energies to anything other than the task in hand. Never once, as we emerged from the celebrations was I conscious that by my actions any Roman Catholic had any more reason to feel less safe or secure. We were not perfect; of course we made the traditional tribal noises and gestures, but strictly on a purely impersonal level. We were at times guilty of being emotionally immature, this often rose out of a strong sense of frustration. This was usually invoked when there was any possibility of the celebrations being threatened by bad weather. On these occasions we were usually inclined to accuse the Roman Catholics of having a hotline to Him who has the power to send the sun to shine and the rain to fall on the just as well as the unjust. When we became overzealous and emotional in our festivities we had a very appropriate safety valve, and this brought us into contact with the only real personality (apart from King Billy) to popularize the celebrations. This was a venerable old gentleman of foreign descent who resided thousands of miles away and who was probably just as hazy concerning the role thrust upon him in our own particular set-up as we were of him, knowing him only as a four-lettered word. Yet around that time of the year you could say with a certain amount of truth and justification that for such a distant relationship he enjoyed quite the greater part of our thoughts.

Two things in my early infancy puzzled my young Protestant mind regarding the Pope. A recess at the top of our street had been bricked up in such a way that it was easy to imagine that something or other had been entombed within. I often wondered what persistent childhood questions of mine regarding it had prompted the answer which was to leave a lasting impression on me; 'the Pope is buried in there.' I never passed that recess without sparing a thought for the Pope, incarcerated inside. From the first faltering attempts at recognizing words and putting sentences together I was also intrigued by the statements so liberally written over our gable walls 'No Pope Here'. This confused me no end and was regarded by me almost in the same context as a later craze which sprang up all over Belfast concerning that mysterious character Skiboo. Skiboo was here or there or had been here, or quite plainly not here at all. Was the Pope like Skiboo? Someone who only lived in our imagination, existing only in the mind of the person who created him? It must be apparent that my education had been sadly lacking.

When we did not make the journey to the field at Finaghy, we usually took up position on a perimeter wall with our backs to what is now the Queen's University School of Medical Biology. The view from the wall was excellent and we sat captivated by the performance.

Much has changed from the Twelfth procession of my youth. Many well-known bands have gone for one thing, and along with them the spectator participation which they engendered. It was hard to keep from singing to those stirring tunes they blazed out. The great tunes of the First World War era: 'Pack up your Troubles', 'Goodbye Dolly', 'Take me back to dear Old Blighty' and, of course, 'Tipperary'. Then there was the great variety of music hall songs that had us all singing and tapping our feet: 'Lily of La-guna', 'Peggy O'Neill' and 'Little Dolly Day Dream', to name but a few, with the 'Sash' being the favourite.

It was always a thrill and did your heart good to listen to two groups, one on each side of the band, singing as they marched along the pavement such songs as 'All the nice girls love a Sailor'. One of the more recent bands I always watched out for was the Regal Accordion, complete with saxophones its repertoire included a large number of old and current favourites. Then there were the old stalwarts like the Shaftesbury, the Ulster Amateurs and the Reid Memorial, and many others too numerous to mention. But nothing affected me as completely, or had my young heart tingling with a feeling of pride and belonging more, than to hear the Ormeau Military or such like take to the hill the sound of 'Soldiers of the Queen'. Perhaps the fault lies in the keenness of my youth, I am not sure, but somehow my fondest memories of the Twelfth belong to the past.

The tumult and the shouting dies. The captains and the kings depart. After the final ember had grown cold and the last collarette carefully shed and the rhythmic sound of snuffling feet and brass and drum lived only as a warm but stored memory, it was then, judged with the over-demanding enthusiasm of younger hearts, that the remainder of the day existed only as an anticlimax, the atmosphere reminding me of a Sunday, quiet, respectable and ever so solemn-looking. We had expected to be caught up in a crescendo of endless merrymaking and revelry when suddenly it had died to an inaudible whisper.

Chapter 7

Sunday and My Premature Awareness

Probably an accurate commentary on our Sunday was that expressed by the cartoonist when he illustrated the plane flying over Belfast from which the pilot had to bail out. The only snag was the parachute refused to open; below was the caption 'Nothing ever opens in Belfast on a Sunday.' Not that the Sundays of my youth were dull, far from it. We just approached our amusements from another angle, saw them in a different setting from that of through the week. We were prepared to clothe them with an air of respectability. Football gave way to street games, everything was entered into with one dominant thought in mind: we were clothed in our Sunday best. However modest, we had to treat our Sunday best with a certain degree of care; everybody who had one wore his navy blue suit on that special day.

When I was a lad I went with my dad,
And we always got clad at Spackmans.
Now I am a dad with many a lad
And we still get clad at Spackmans.[8]

My father at that time, though not an active member of any church, was at heart a deeply religious man and a fairly strict sabbatarian. The unwritten rule for that day was always rigidly adhered to, namely that anything which could possibly be done the day previous, should be carried out accordingly. He refused to discuss anything relating to the future on a Sunday, always saying that this is not the proper day to make plans. On Sunday, as far as the wireless was concerned, the world still waited on the genius of Marconi. Because of this, I always made a point of visiting my married sister when I knew she would be listening to *King Solomon's Mines*, a series in which I had a keen interest. Another favourite of mine was *Happidrome* – 'We three in Happidrome, working for the B.B.C., Ramsbottom, Enoch and Me.' But my real favourite was the midweek broadcast of *Appointment with Fear*, with Valentine Dyall as The Man in Black, with his super-silky sinister voice.

I can recall one late Autumn evening listening to his programme completely on my own. It was not dark enough to have the light on but still not clear enough to prevent the

---

[8] This was used in an advert for a men's outfitters on the High Street.

shadows cast by our fire from improvising their own choreography on the walls of our kitchen. I remember how he introduced his stories something like this. 'This is your storyteller, the man in black. Turn out the light and pull your chair a little closer to the fire. Take a last look around you for our story tonight is the bizarre tale of "The Monkey's Paw".' The shadows on our wall were really working overtime as was the pulse rate of my poor thumping heart. Even a hasty poke of the fire failed to disperse them and only succeeded in drawing my attention to the small lump of coal sticking to one of the bars of our grate. Always an unmistakable sign, according to my mother, that we were sure to have a visit from a stranger! Long before the son, who was but a few days buried, returned from 'that undiscovered country from whose bourne no traveller returns', I had vacated the premises. But life, if it has taught anything, has convinced me that we have nothing to fear from the dead.

I was now twelve years old and had, like most boys of my age at that time lived a robust but fairly sheltered life. I was not unaware or unresponsive to the attractions of the opposite sex, having formed many a healthy and normal relationship with my female counterparts. When I was a little older, I remember waiting in a queue for a trolley bus. It was just after visiting two of my aunts, I was feeling extremely happy and well pleased with myself, sentiments which followed that day and upon every visit to their home. Although, during the visits, there was a certain amount of personal discomfort experienced. That day, they freely commented to one another on how I had grown my looks and family mannerisms, often comparing me to a favourite nephew of theirs. From this they switched to my personal relationships with the fairer sex, how many girls I had and did I kiss them. These adulatory overtures I suffered in silence, accepting them as the natural outpourings of two females who had seen their family aspire to adulthood around them and then disappear. Besides the final outcome of their deliberations, they would always offer me a very generous sum of money which eventually reached me after I had made the customary protestations, and they on their part had threatened on its non-acceptance to end any further communication between us. Until I, the hypocrite that I was, rather reluctantly occurred. I always left their house indoctrinated into feeling like a paragon of virtue and God's gift to lonely females.

Quite abruptly while I waited for a trolley bus to fetch me back to normality, I was confronted by myself in the window of a shop opposite. The effect was startling, it seemed suddenly apparent that I had outgrown my shorts almost to the point of the burlesque – like an adult pretending to be a schoolboy. I was conscious of a need to cover the nakedness of my legs, to get home as quickly as I could and hide myself, at least until I was able to conform to my conspicuous physical maturity, so dramatically revealed to me by sliding down the bannisters (to use a colloquialism for an

102

initial conversion into long pants). The effect on me was unsought and I felt unprepared. I had been confronted with an unexpected sense of maturity in advance of my years. I could never be the same again. I had weighed up the situation and made a rational decision, and whether I liked it or not, in so doing I had emerged that much more worldly-wise. But my premature awareness of the powerful desires and emotions of the physical world around me was something which I quite happily locked away in a drawer of my personal life, marked Private, for future reference only.

Chapter 8

The Battler from the Back Streets and Football

VE Day had passed into history and in our books and comics the Germans had momentarily retired from the scene. The Japanese forces were the men who popularized our reading material and Rockfist Rogan of *The Champion*, the boxer-come-air ace, having finished off the Germans in Europe, had now turned his attention to the Pacific. On the celluloid screen John Wayne was at his best fighting the war in the Pacific, but VE Day could not be surpassed and winning had become a more or less commonplace sort of thing. So much so that VJ Day found me coolly and calmly at camp in Dunmurry, on the outskirts of Belfast. Already in my youthful imagination, with an end to hostilities, somehow or other the glamour of the Legion and Royal Navy fast receded into the background and soon faded from the scene altogether.

Around this time, as we gradually learnt to adjust our lives, now no longer seen in the context of a global confrontation, I was greatly influenced by a story in *The Wizard*, one of my favourite boy's comics. Each week I received *The Hotspur* previously ordered for me by my mother along with *The Beano* and *The Dandy* from Nelson's shop at the corner of Sandy Row. After reading *The Hotspur* I eagerly swapped it with one of my chums for his *Wizard* containing the story which I faithfully followed each week, 'The Battler from the Back Streets'. Here was a character with whom I could easily identify, without resorting to any great stretch of my imagination: a young boy well down the social scale, born in poverty, from the back streets of a great city, who each week was seen rising further away from obscurity, and nearer to fame and fortune all with the help of his fighting fists. It was an old story but a popular one and greatly fired the imagination of the youth of our day. After all it was a story with sound basis in fact, being acted out in the real world about us. Boxing at the end of the war had received a new lease of life and such popular heroes as Freddie Mills rose to fame via the boxing booths, born out of the interest created in boxing during the aftermath of the war.

On the local scene such names as Jimmy Warnock. Spider Kelly, Tommy Armour, Bunty Doran and Rinty Monaghan were bywords in the days of my youth, although some of them had passed their peak even then. I read, marked, learnt and inwardly digested everything to do with the fight game. My most treasured possessions were the monthly magazine of *The Ring*, sent to me religiously from America by my Uncle Gordon Skelly, which I suppose was some form of compensation for having his name incorporated into mine at my christening.

A popular pastime in those days was to exchange the names and addresses of film stars, the end result of which, after some correspondence, the starry-eyed fan ended up the proud possessor of a glossy photograph signed personally by the star. Many a time I had seen such photographs as Clark Gable, Robert Taylor, Betty Grable, and Judy Garland (the Rainbow Girl), change hands. But for me, my idols were probably less amorous, not as photogenic, but no less stars in their own right with their own special claim to fame and fortune. I had surrounded myself with pictures and photographs, too numerous to name individually, but to mention only a few at random, Joe Louis, Henry Armstrong, Jack Johnston, Stanley Ketchal, Jack Demspey, Jim Driscoll, Mel Tarleton and Benny Lynch, the list is endless. For me the photograph which took pride of place among such a galaxy of stars was our own Jimmy Warnock. This I placed at my bedside along with a photograph of him and his brothers, taken after a sparring session at the Old Beresford Club on the Shankill Road.

Another boxing story which influenced me greatly was the one I often heard my father relate about the Black Prince, the famous Jack Peterson. How as a quiet and rather reserved young lad living in a district in which such qualities were seen as a sign of weakness, his father felt compelled to have him taught in the noble art of self-defence. Thus began his first steps upon the rung of the ladder of fame.

Our district lent a certain contribution to the fight game in the post-war era through a man who had his wee corner shop in our area, at the corner of Blondin Street and Napier Street (now occupied in a similar capacity as a grocer's shop by the Clark family). His later claim to popularity as a boxing promoter came about after he left our district, though while in the corner shop his interest in boxing went without saying, evidence of which was seen in the many photographs and correspondence from boxers past and present which adorned his shop. Though being too young to know him other than through the eyes of a child, I can still picture Bobby Gardiner coming out of his shop complete with white apron always ready for a game of street football with the lads. My father was also a keen boxing fan. I remember him and I on a Saturday evening, queueing outside the Ulster Hall from 5.30 p.m., and the bill itself not starting until 8.00 p m., the doors not opening until 7.00 p m. This early arrival enabled us to occupy our favourite seats in the middle front row of the balcony overlooking the ring. Here we saw such locals as Bunty Devan, Gerry Smyth, Tommy Armour, Jim Keery, Ike Weir, Paddy Dowdall and Joe Bay Collins, the last two both from the Republic of Ireland. All gave of their best. Many a pilgrimage I made to what was once the

Mecca of boxing, the King's Hall, with interest at that time so high that even locals like Gerry Smyth and Jim Keery topped the bill. Here I would sit outside among the boxing fraternity, queueing from 4.50 p.m. for a bill which did not begin until 8.00 p.m., enthralled by the local gossip surrounding the gladiators who were about to perform, feasting on the atmosphere of what, for me, was the greatest of all sports. So dedicated was I, that I had even taken my grandfather to see the film of the Sugar Ray Robinson and Randolph Turpin fight in the Royal Hippodrome. He came from Ballyhill (and had at one time slaughtered pigs for a living), and was a keen boxing fan with a memory stretching back to the times he was a professional soldier in the Boer War. It seemed my keenness knew no bounds even sitting up twice to catch the Jersey Joe Walcott and Joe Louis fight at 3.00 a.m., as on the previous occasion the fight was called off due to bad weather. With such a keen interest it was inevitable that I should become actively involved in the sport itself.

Football was at this time only of secondary interest to me and that in the capacity of a spectator only, never feeling at any time that my talents lay in that direction, apart from street football, which of course I involved myself in wholeheartedly, but as a pastime only and not from any aspirations to greatness. Coming from Sandy Row I was of course an avid Linfield supporter and for me my greatest thrill as a football fan was to see Celtic and the Blues battle it out.

What an action-packed ninety minutes of a-thrill-a-minute, supercharged atmosphere these two contributed to. My favourite personalities of these games, were strangely enough the two goalkeepers, Alex Russell and Hughie Kelly. In the true spirit of teamsmanship, I would watch these two spur on their respective teams to greater efforts. Alex was the true professional in his own quiet but firm way, while Hughie was the star of the show with all the usual theatricals of a great player as he pranced and danced along the goal line, shouting his head off, not forgetting to cross himself at the start of each match, amid the howls of verbal abuse directed at him from the terraces. He was unafraid to show his disapproval and annoyance at a Linfield goal by taking it out on his cap. He was but one of a number of great personalities who dominated the game in those days.

Coming from the excitement and glamour of such a match as the big two our arrival home signalled a quick bite to eat, or as my father would say, 'A run around the table and a kick at the cat.' How often had my mother's council led me to slow it down, as I gulped my food down, anxious to get away? It was as if we were afraid that some of the enthusiasm and inspiration which had rubbed off on us from the match would disappear and we were determined to show our faces before this occurred. It was remarkable how spontaneously we appeared at the street corner. Within a matter of minutes we were shedding some of our surplus energy and finding an outlet for our enthusiasm as, individually, we relived the match, each one of us in the privacy of his own thoughts imagining himself to be whatever hero that afternoon had taken his particular fancy. With it being a Saturday evening we would continue playing until it was time for the second house in the pictures. All our football was not confined to the street corners of Sandy Row, some of the happiest days of my youth, when I was between thirteen and sixteen, were experienced playing football at Belvoir Estate with my chums, on the many weekends we retired there during the summer.

Chapter 9
The Graves at Belvoir

At Belvoir, situated along the Lagan, in a field already prepared by us for that purpose, we played football and cricket setting up our camp along the banks of a tributary of the river. In an atmosphere designed to captivate the most unimaginative schoolboy, we allowed ourselves the luxury of indulging in the most ghoulish fantasies and weird situations it was possible for our over-fertile minds to create. The estate itself was surrounded by a huge wall easily two to three feet thick. A main path led into the estate, on either side of which were trees and vegetation of every description. The main path itself suddenly ended in a maze of little paths all reaching out further and deeper into the vegetation, like the long tentacles of a giant squid. One of the little paths rearing to the left, when followed to its ultimate conclusion, suddenly and without any warning, brought you into the burial ground of the estate. Here were graves dating back over two hundred years, going way back into the eighteenth century. The graveyard itself followed no recognizable boundary, having become almost identified with the surrounding vegetation. Very few of the headstones had remained in a vertical position, and those that had were mostly swallowed up by the earth as if she were intent to keep their secret safe from prying eyes. The stones in a horizontal position were most easily read, with headstones clearly marked as dating from the eighteenth century. Not far away was a tomb with an inscription clearly dating it back to the same century. It was the tomb of the Viscount Dungannon. During the same time as our visits to the estate quite a lot of local interest was raised, receiving headline news in the *Belfast Telegraph*, following the desecration of the tomb and the stealing of the two lead coffins.

Deep into the heart of Belvoir, on a hill commanding a magnificent view to the south, taking in that immediate part of the Lagan as it converged on the estate, lay the great Georgian mansion, even after all these years still clothed in the splendour of yesteryear, its structure boldly defiant against the onslaughts of wind and rain.[9] The evening sun projected its shadow against the hill, unaltered since its structure, born in the mind of the architect, was completed

---

[9] The house was demolished by the Forest Service in 1961. We must presume that the army used explosives to blow it up, as a training exercise.

all those years ago. It was zealously guarded by a game-keeper, armed with a shotgun that discharged pellets sadistically coated in salt to deter any unwelcome visitors.

Due to its strategic position it was only on very rare occasion that we dared to visit the mansion, and then not without a lot of reconnaissance beforehand. As it was situated on a hill surrounded by large lawns stretching down to the rising vegetation encircling the estate, it was almost impossible to approach it without being observed during the hours of daylight. Many a night I had peered out from within this circle of vegetation, pondering over what sinister secret lurked within its dark halls, so tenaciously guarded by the gamekeeper. To view it as we had done around the midnight hour was quite an experience with the moon playing hide and seek among the dark clouds of the night sky, and the tomb of the Viscount not too far to the rear of us. The rustling and crackling in the undergrowth around us in the stillness of the night, like sounds picked up on a hidden amplifier, was all clearly indicative of the nocturnal activities of the creatures who scurried to and fro, while every now and then, as if to remind us that we had invaded the privacy of his hunting hour, came the feathered activity among the branches overhead of the night owl, and his oral disapproval of our midnight activities. Often my heart had skipped a beat at the sudden nearness of these woodland creatures as they busily engaged themselves in their nightly pursuits.

Deeper into the forest as it began to descend to the tributary of the Lagan, near to the location of our camp, was the ice house belonging to the mansion. A little path, now barely recognizable, but at closer scrutiny clearly visible, trodden in by centuries of traffic, connected the ice house and the mansion. As I stood in the vicinity of the ice house I would let my imagination take me back to those far off days of snuff and powdered wigs. To me it seemed as if across the centuries I could hear the servants discussing, at second-hand, the main topics of conversation of the gentry discussed over dinner at the big house: the American War of Independence; the latest ballyhoo over the *Paul Jones*, an American frigate's intrusion into the Belfast Lough. Years later it would be the French Revolution – give them cake indeed. The proletariat had given them cake alright, whatever was the world coming to? The estate was loaded with atmosphere. It seemed to hang heavy in the air to which, it must be added, we made our own contribution by devising our own theatrical props which were our attempts to create atmosphere of a more frightening kind, for this we turned to the films.

The arch villain of the films in those days, by Boris Karloff, was of course Bela Lugosi, who brilliantly portrayed Bram Stoker's *Dracula* to perfection. It was he who had us gripping our seats and looking over our shoulders on a dark night, discussing whether there were really such things as vampires (sub-humans) who existed by living on the blood of their victims. I will never forget the thrill of seeing him live on stage in the Belfast Opera House accompanied by the Bangor Amateur Dramatic Society, even his verbal introduction to the story of *Dracula* had the hallmark of the professional as the spotlight suddenly picked out this lone figure standing on the stage. No elaborate make-up, certainly no artificial props, the magnificence of the man was caught in his eyes and voice. There was a quiet reverent hush over the audience, which in itself was strange (I myself had seen many a big star become actively involved in a change of hostilities with this same audience), but here was the true master at work. One was left feeling perhaps there was something really sinister about this man, maybe he was, after all, in league with the forces of evil.

In a small clearing, not far from where the main path divided, we had dug a slip trench, representing a grave, hidden from the rising sun and into which we had driven a stake, the symbols of the human vampire. I can still see Davy Gibson, Big Dickie Allen, Jackie Todd and me coming out of the second house of the Curzon on a Saturday night and heading for our weekend camp at Belvoir, which we had set up the previous night. The atmosphere was terrific as we made our way along the main path on a dark summer's night, approaching the midnight hour. Being the youngest of the quartet I would catch my breath as the bats swooped around our heads and some of our party made the obvious association between them and Dracula. My thoughts turned to the solitary grave dug and staked when someone would echo audibly the wild fantasies filling my head as we approached the spot where the grave lay hidden in the undergrowth. Supposing some supernatural force had accepted our bravado in digging the grave as an open invitation and filled it? What if some real live vampire had retired there for the night? Perhaps we were trifling with the forces of evil, the power of which we did not fully understand. Davy, sceptical as usual, would give a laugh at this, but the bats whizzing past us emitting their own strange sounds, coupled with the rise and fall of the water from the weir and our own sharp footfalls on the hard pathway, echoing back to us from the depths of the forest, did nothing to reassure us. We continued on into the depths of the forest until we came to our camp, situated along the riverbank. As our first task we lit a fire to protect us from the 'Beastie and things that go bump in the night'. Actually I was of the opinion that the fire attracted the beasties, namely our rodent neighbours, with whom we shared the riverbank, who seemed to have devised a game of dare among themselves as to which of them could get nearest the fire without us detecting them. In consequence we set watch of an hour and a half each. To me the whole set-up resembled the experience one has of going on the ghost train as a child, when such opposing adjectives as awful, smashing, never again, great, and scared out of our wits, are all used to describe the same experience. This was the Belvoir we knew best and accepted as such. But for me the real character of Belvoir will always be Freddie, who lived in the next street to me in the Row.

It was he who introduced most of us to Belvoir. He, more than anyone, had entered into the true spirit and atmosphere of the place. To see him stride out of the undergrowth equipped with his gun, sporting gumboots into which were tucked corduroy trousers, and clad in a buckskin-type jacket over which two bandoleers were strung in criss-cross fashion, topped off with Davy Crocket-type headwear made from rabbit skins, was a never-to-be-forgotten experience. To me he resembled a frontiersman straight out of some plot created for him by no less a person than Daniel Defoe. I almost expected to hear the war cry of the Mohicans in his wake. He was our trail scout and we were content to sit at his feet in admiration. Guided by Freddie's experience and energy we even had our own private bathing pool, a little shallow pool of water which had become isolated from the main tributary and which on a summer's day was the equivalent to a heated indoor pool.

The large fields which we had marked off as our sports area were in the most ideal surroundings, beginning as they did at the edge of a forest of large rhododendrons stretching right down to the river's edge, whose ancestors must at one time had graced the Himalayan and Smoky mountain ranges, and whose very presence was clear evidence of the far-reaching attempts at cultivation emanating from the one time predecessors of this Georgian edifice. Here, completely oblivious of calculated time, we spent many happy hours from sunrise to sunset. Now Belvoir as I knew it has almost disappeared, the mansion has gone altogether, succumbed to the bulldozer and the onward march of progress. Some of my best friends, who allowed me to share their experience of Belvoir with them, have also gone. But the experience which I shared with them still remains and will remain with them even after I am gone, and this after all, I suppose, is a milestone on the road to man's quest for immortality.

Chapter 10
Victory Boxing Club

At thirteen like most boys of my age, I was tingling all over with the freshness and excitement of life, physically fit and full of beans. It seemed that I approached everything in top gear, every street crossing became a challenge to me as with a sudden burst of speed I would see how many strides I could take the next street crossing in. With my healthy body and keen interest in boxing it was inevitable that I should, as I have said, become actively involved in the sport. After persistent appeals to be allowed to join some club or other, and a bit of head-scratching on the part of my father as to the best means of accomplishing this (he had mentioned that he knew Archie Anderson, trainer of the Crown Amateur Boxing Club), it was soon discovered that an uncle of mine had friends who were associated with the fight game. As a result of this I was taken by my uncle to a sister of his who owned a shop in Cupar Street. Her husband was somehow connected with a local boxing club.

Eventually her husband and I finally arrived at the Victory Boxing Club, Shankill Road.

My first impressions of the interior were all I could possibly have imagined a boxing club to be; it was only with experience that I realized some of its shortcomings. Still it was all that I had wished for, with a tradition incorporating my local hero, Jimmy Warnock, when it was known as the Old Beresford. The club itself was situated over the Long Bar on the Shankill Road and approached by an entry type opening in off the main road leading into a cobblestoned courtyard which was itself a cul-de-sac and thereby providing a side entrance to the pub, which also contained a bookmakers shop. The only approach to the club was from this yard via a wooden flight of stairs erected independently of the building, zigzagging in fire escape fashion and stretching from the yard to the loft-like opening at the top. The club had one main room which was the proper gym. Another room, which in actual fact was the roof space of the building entered from the gym by a tiny ladder through an opening made in the floor, was used as the dressing room. The gym was well equipped. There were punch bags, a punch ball, floor to ceiling balls, and a fair amount of space for skipping. The centre was occupied by that geometrical contradiction, the square ring: that small arena which separates the men from the boys. The prevalent smell of the whole place was a combination of sweat and Sloan's liniment. The walls of the gym were painted with cartoon-like characters of boxers during the different stages of their training, one example being of a boxer throwing a punch which connects with the punch ball and which he fails to avoid on its return swing; the next we see of him he is rather distressed-looking, depending on the piece of equipment he had just been using to hold himself up, a circle of stars decorating his head like a halo and his eyes having that going away look. A man in a roll-neck sweater, holding a watch bawled out to the boxers, using the gym at different periods of time 'Last half and last ten'. The response of the boxers to this was to put a greater sense of speed and urgency into their training. The dressing room's main items of furniture were a large wooden table used for massaging the boxers and a number of wooden forms spread around the sides of the loft. A collection of nails hammered into the wooden beams of the roof served, ideally, as coat hangers. The two trainers in charge of the club when I arrived were Billy Barnes and Billy Brett. For roadwork we met Billy Barnes and Billy Brett on a Sunday morning at 7.00 a.m. at the corner of Agnes Street. Fitted out in heavy boots and sweaters, we started walking briskly as far as the West Circular Road, where we broke into a trot, running right around the West Circular as far as the Whiterock. Up the hill at the Whiterock we were expected to run backwards, aided and abetted by Billy Brett, who kept throwing stones at anyone he discovered cheating. Once we had arrived at the summit we commenced a series of exercises. We completed our training at the club where Barney gave a shower to anyone who was prepared to stand naked out in the cobblestoned courtyard while he directed a jet of cold water from a hosepipe, as he stood on the stairs outside the club.

Before I parted company with the club, we had a brand new shower installed in our dressing room. As a young lad I soon learnt, from our training sessions at the club, the matter of fact and utter frankness with which we accepted the naked body. There was no time for any prudery. I remember standing clothed only in my towel, which I had fastened around me like a kilt after finishing a training session, the next thing I knew it was whisked off me and I was left standing in my birthday suit while the trainer proceeded to dry me down, and then with a word of command (everything seemed to be at the double) he had me turning around in a pirouette, while he fanned me with my towel.

Another thing I learnt was perseverance. My poor knuckles were in raw flesh, both from softness and failure to punch correctly. No sooner had they healed up, but they broke out again, and I had not even been in the ring for a sparring session. So much for the glamour of the fight game. Some of the cures I was given to harden my hands were unbelievable and most unhygienic, but with the proper training and perseverance my hands healed and hardened up to the extent that I never, at any time, either in or out of the ring, used bandages to protect them. Two and sometimes three nights a week my life revolved around the club over the Long Bar. It was an experience which I would not have missed for all the tea in China. Here as a lad at first-hand I had a chance to see some of the big men, and the not so big, the great and the not so great, the dedicated and the not so dedicated.

My first fight outside the Victory, where we ran many shows in which we were visited by outside clubs, took me to the Rialto at Peters Hill. What an experience that turned out to be. It seemed, as I sat stripped in the dressing room waiting to go on, that all hell was let loose in the corridor outside. All during the time I attended the club, and that was up until I was sixteen, I weighed just below the eight stone mark – I was quite a small lad really. Suddenly the dressing room doors burst open and in dances this big fellow, whom I had seen a few minutes earlier shadow boxing in front of me in the dressing room before he went on. He had certainly impressed me anyway, being proportionally twice my size, now here he was yelling blue murder, surrounded by two or three men all frantically, but unsuccessfully, trying to quieten him. The nearer they came to him the harder he yelled. He was almost inarticulate. Crikey, I thought, what had they done to him? They must be murdering each other out there. I must confess at this point to feeling strange goings on in my stomach. This experience has been described as being synonymous with the flutter of butterflies, but to keep to the same analogy I must say it rather seemed as if someone was in hot pursuits of these same butterflies, whose tiny wings were going a mile a minute, being pursued by a man with hobnail boots on. This I think is a closer description of how I felt, as the big fellow kept pointing to his shoulder as more officials piled into the dressing room. Without any warning one of them grabbed the big fellow's hand and gave his arm a jerk. I thought there and then that the big fellow must have been a sailor at one time; the language that ushered forth from him at this sudden activity of the official must have taken in at least three or four languages. But it had the desired result. His shoulder, which had been dislocated, was jerked into its socket again.

In a way the incident reminded me of the story my father loved to tell of when a famous boxer came over here to box some up-and-coming Irishman (I forget his name). On the night of the fight there were many outside the hall who had been unable to purchase a ticket as the fight was a sell-out, but who all wanted to hear the result. Some wise guy arriving late for the fight, with his brand new ticket, the envy of all who watched him, approached the inside entrance to the hall and became the receiver of information relating to what was happening inside. He turned on his heel and addressed himself to the crowd outside, 'Does anybody want to buy a ticket? It's terrible in there, why they're simply murdering one another and my stomach couldn't stand it, someone should stop it.' Of course the gentleman is rushed in the process, the highest bidder purchasing the ticket. The guy rushes into the hall only to meet Mickey Walker coming out of the dressing rooms ready to leave having already polished off his man in the first round.

Once when we went to box at Malone Training Home, at the invitation of Billy Wright who was the Home's training instructor and also trained at our gym, I became the unwitting accomplice to an incident were one inmate worked over another. The fights were in progress and I had come out of the room we were using as a dressing room, into the short hallway immediately outside our own room. As I did so I noticed a lad dressed in the home uniform lounging in the hallway, then up comes this other lad similarly dressed. Seeing me he asks the question 'Are there any masters in the long hallway?' Quite obligingly I left the short hallway we were standing in and went to the junction where it was continued by the long hall. In perfect innocence, I peered round the corner and replied in the negative. It was the signal for fisticuffs to begin. Without any warning, he attacked this lad in as neat a fashion as any professional. Within moments the lounger was rolling on the floor holding his stomach and yelling to high heaven, his attacker having disappeared in a flash, leaving me completely bewildered by the whole thing. Attracted by the yelling, a master came running up the hallway brandishing a cane. At first I thought he was heading straight for me, but ignoring me and extracting the required information from the recipient of this attack he went off in hot pursuit of the attacker. I later learnt that the lad who had been the victim of the attack was supposed to have grassed to the masters about something or other.

Our boxing activities were not only confined to the Belfast area but took us all around the country. On these occasions we did not go as our own particular club, but as a group of individuals, all from various clubs from around the Belfast area. The comradeship was good and I made quite a number of friends from across the religious divide. On the outings after the serious business of the evening was over we really enjoyed ourselves. After one such outing where we had been boxing at St. Marys Hall Newcastle, we received a slap-up meal afterwards in the Slieve Donard Hotel. The crack and the singing afterwards in the bus were always my happiest memories of these boxing excursions. Coming back on the bus, I can still see this big man, Wilson, a really jovial character who had retired from boxing but was now a referee. I think he was trainer to the Lower Shankill. Wilson took a cork from a refreshing bottle for the return journey, lit it with a match and, when it was sufficiently burnt, proceeded to have his face made-up to pretend he had black eyes. He put another cork in his mouth, giving the effect of a swollen face, his intentions being, on arriving home, to tell the wife we had been short for the bill and he had to fill the breach.

Boxing in those days provided me with a passport into areas which I normally would not have frequented. Like the night after a show when I was walking home with this well-known amateur heavy, who later turned professional but whose name I can't recall. He was still wearing his signet, on which was emblazoned the Sacred Heart, the emblem of his club. He led us out through the Joy Street area where, to my surprise, we called at the home of another old professional favourite of mine still in business in those days, Tommy Madine. Boxing was an ideal ambassador for good relations.

One thing I have omitted to state is the part my father played in all this. I was now fifteen and my father, realizing that my involvement had not been a passing fancy on my part, began to take a closer interest in the whole proceedings, seeing himself I believe, as my self-appointed manager. This came home to me when we crossed town to take part in a show at St. Matthew's Hall, Seaford Street. My father usually took up his seat in these locations with the minimum of communication with me, but this particular night he came right into our dressing room enquiring of me who I was down to box. This amazed me but I gave him the necessary information and he left immediately. Coming back later to the door of our dressing room he engaged my attention and then, with a side jerk of the head, called me over to him. It all seemed so very secretive and hush hush, standing by me and gazing all around, as if he was either approving or disapproving of our dressing room facilities, and at the same time giving a friendly nod to Charlie Brown, one of the lads from our club who was preparing to go on, all the while speaking out of the side of his mouth. He said, 'This fellow,' (he stopped for a minute to look me over) 'is a big lad, I've just seem him stripped and from what I have been able to learn, he likes a scrap.' I was not used to this kind of treatment and though entered into with the best intentions in the world, to my own psychological make-up, it was very off-putting to say the least. I preferred leaving the fighting till I got into the ring, a dedicated convert to the philosophy of 'what you don't know does you no harm'. But he continued on 'Yeas a big fellow, they say he likes to make a rough house of it. One thing though, I have learnt, which we can use to our advantage, the ring tilts.' My amazement knew no bounds at this, half expecting him to say something like, 'our only salvation is if the ring collapses,' but he carried on with tilts of the head in the direction of the hall. 'We can counteract his height by holding to that part of the ring furthermost away from the audience and which will give you a certain amount of increased height.' All this seemed a very valid point from my 'new manager', but one thing he omitted to take into consideration was the lad I was due to fight belonged to St. Matthews, so this was his home territory. My happiest memories of boxing belong to that night and with the reaction I received from some of the audience. I can still see my father and brother both on their feet shouting me on. It was an especially happy time for me when I think of how relations were strained between them at that particular time. But there they were, both showing a common front identified as one, in their enthusiasm.

It was not long after this I was to stand at my brother's bedside as he lay dying, doing my best to choke back the tears as they came. Trying, in that one moment, to act like someone who has behind him an adult experience stretching over a lifetime, but ending up looking like someone who is quite obviously out of his depth. I was just a raw kid faced with a situation I could not understand: a young man in the prime of life dying. My brother, seeing my obvious distress, put his hand in mine and used a metaphor from boxing, which for me has made every single moment spent under the shadow of the square ring and every punch on the chin worthwhile, 'now we will have none of that, for I know you can take it on the chin.'

It was sometime after his death, when my boxing activities once more had me on the move (this time to the heart of Belfast's docklands for the St. John Basco's Club on Corporation Street), that the full impact of his words hit me. I was now sixteen and, though I did not know it at the time, my boxing career, inauspicious though it may have been, was coming to an abrupt end. In fact the 'Battler from the Back Streets' was already fighting a battle he did not know about and one which he was destined to lose: the battle for his health. Already I was feeling abnormally tired. Something written up on the Basco's club hall, following on from what my brother had said to me, was to fortify me in the battle of life we call living. Someone had painted on a large mirror in the St. John Basco's gym the following exhortation, 'Look boys, you have got to be able to take it.' I think Jesus must have meant something like that when He said to His disciples, 'If any man come after me, he must deny himself, take up his cross and follow me.'[10] Deny himself, forget about self-pity, take up his cross, realize his shortcomings and by the time he may have done this, the shock may have put him on the canvas. But comes the call 'follow me'. The only way we can do that is to give our heads a shake and get up from the deck. You see, all the trimmings of the gym and all the professional chit-chat which surround it are geared but with one purpose in mind, the ultimate performance in the ring, and it was there in the ring that I learnt one of life's most important lessons, the necessity which comes to all of us at one time or another, to stand alone. It may be in the face of some adversity, or in the interests of some cause, but the ring is one place the bully boys of this world stay clear of, and you can't kick a man when he is down. There the rules are geared so that only the referee decides if a boxer has had enough. The winning usually is only a matter of mathematics, in the long run the manner of taking part is the all-important thing.

---

[10] Luke 9:23.

Chapter 11

"It"

Now over sixteen, I was conscious of tremendous pressures probably related to each other, both spiritual and physical, all demanding recognition. The physical were more in evidence as I became increasingly aware of the extra efforts required of me even in my normal training sessions. Much of the zip and zest had gone and physical activities in the gym which I normally took in my stride now found me labouring at with great difficulty. Deep-rooted guilt complexes which one usually associates with an emergence into adolescence were also making their presence felt. Now no longer capable of sustaining any consistent interest in the club, my attitudes became confused and certainly incapable of being identified with what my true feelings were. As a result, at this point of my life I became very unsettled and dissatisfied, both with myself and my job. It seemed as if I was reaching out for something (or other), the object of which I was not fully aware. Like a man reaching out for a light switch in a dark room, the geography of which he is totally unfamiliar, with a sort of quest for a meaning and purpose to life in common with so many young people in a similar situation, I finally reached out not for the light switch whose location was a matter of trial and error, but I suppose more predictably towards a more familiar source of energy, a word from the beyond for our human predicament. This new found faith was something which was to help and sustain me before and during a long period of illness. For having ignored at my peril the inner voice of nature, ever endeavouring to warn me all was not well, I found myself admitted to Musgrave Park hospital, seriously ill. The first time I became aware of how ill I really was, happened one morning at the moment of waking when I discovered that I had been bleeding internally, from the mouth. Very soon after I had a haemorrhage and was immediately rushed to hospital. This was a few weeks before Christmas 1951, and I was at the ripe old age of sixteen. That all was far from well soon became evident as I realized that people around me were not so much talking directly to me, but at me through one another. Whispered comments like 'He's so young-looking too', and words like neglect came filtering through to my consciousness.

After I had spent a few weeks in hospital, a young lady doctor came to see me. Sitting on my bed she began to explain to me something of the nature of my illness and what would be expected of me. For one thing, I was to be moved to another ward. Apparently I had contracted tuberculosis, one of the then major killer diseases in the United Kingdom. I questioned her about the time factor regarding my recovery and she began talking from the minimum period of a year. I was completely bewildered by all that she was saying. Surely she couldn't be talking about me. I was hoping that at any moment someone would pinch me and this pretty doctor would disappear and I would have awakened as from a bad dream. But this was no dream and the doctor was a real live person as I soon realized when, seeing my obvious despair, she put her arms around me and squeezed me to her, pointing out to me the tremendous strides that medicine had taken in the particular field of my illness. The warmth and depth of feeling which enabled this young Roman Catholic doctor to make physical contact with me was of tremendous therapeutic value for me in my recovery, giving me an admiration for the medical profession which has remained unshaken ever since. From that moment I decided to put myself completely in their hands. She was to prove but one of many, like the Roman Catholic ward sister who nursed me and to whom, like so many of her profession, I was to owe an incalculable debt regarding my eventual recovery.

I soon found that being a patient in a TB ward in those days meant a coming to terms with the realization that time was a factor programmed for each of us in generous quantities, and without any conscious reference to any immediate termination that was always in the future. It was a case of grinning and bearing it or going under; certainly we weren't going anywhere, that was for sure. I had seen too many sign themselves out, having to make the inevitable return, their latter state much worse than their former. It was with this threat of the latter in mind that l had seen our ward sister coming into the ward first thing of a morning and being greeted with louder moans and groans and larger doses of self-pity than usual. She took up her position in the middle of the ward with hands on hips, like a general about to address the troops. From here she reigned supreme, as with a defiant twinkle in her eyes she retorted, 'Have a good look around you; there are no bars on the windows.' She, it was, who kept us on our toes and never spared our feelings. Time and time again she brought us face to face with the realities of our situation, with the necessity to conform and adapt. 'Only those that do this will survive', she would say. She was no lady; this was on her own admission, as she often said if she had been she would never have stuck us so long. She was the complete professional in everything she did, quite often she applied the psychology of an old Music Hall type song:

Don't jump off the roof, Dad
You'll make a hole in the yard
Mother's just planted petunias
The weeding and seeding was hard,
If you must end it all, Dad
Won't you please, give us a break,
Just take a walk down the park, Dad
And there you can jump in the lake.[11]

The lyrics were seen, to a small extent, in the way she administered the injections for the ward. This was a task normally carried out by the nurses but at times, if they were short-staffed, she would take this job upon herself. Most of us being on a long course of injections were unable to take them on our arms and were given them on a more personal part of our anatomy. Nothing was more nerve-wracking than the timorous advances of an inexperienced nurse holding the needle like it was an offensive weapon, fearful of hurting, but by that very fear, destined to make it hard for herself and, at times, the patient. Our ward sister would come into the ward like a whirlwind, picking up the tray and announcing as she did so 'Bottoms up' with a speed and efficiency that was dazzling. Holding the syringe like a dart she had made her point of entry and was gone almost before you had time to adjust your pyjama string.

---

[11] Seymour Cy Coben, 'Don't Jump Off the Roof, Dad', 1961.

One thing I was to learn, our application was no respecter of persons. We were all here from every station in life irrespective of class, or creed: Jew and Gentile, rich man, poor man, beggarman and thief. But once more hands were reaching across the divide to me, this time in the form of a patient next to me. I had just been shifted to this specialist ward though still not fully recovered from my initial experience, and Sean (whom I later learnt came from the Upper Falls area and played for Celtic) made it a point of tucking me in last thing at night and seeing to any last-minute requirements of mine before he retired. His kindness to me is something I shall always remember. There was also the visitation of the many members of the Primitive Street Methodist Church from Sandy Row to which I had become a member previous to my illness.

After a short while in the ward the most depressing thing I discovered, which was to challenge my morale all through my illness, was the high percentage of those patients who had a history of hospitalization at different times and places stretching over a number of years. This was something which I found was almost particularly associated to the working class and which I was determined in my own case to overcome. I set my mind, from the moment I had adjusted myself, to make my stay in hospital as short as humanly possible. To this end, I ate everything set up to me, even porridge which at home I couldn't have looked at let alone eat, especially first thing in the morning. Indeed the most foul-tasting medicine was seen by me as a means to an end and accepted in that spirit.

This fear of having to return was never far from our thoughts. This, I think, was evident in some of the articles we wrote in our ward magazine. As an example, it was usually big news for us when someone was discharged from the ward as being fit to go home. One particular gentleman who was not popular received the usual attention from our magazine but with this difference, some wit had finished off his article on the nagging gentleman with the following double meaning invocation 'and we sincerely hope he will not be back.'

The routine of the ward was set in motion around the unearthly hour of 5.30 a.m. when temperatures were taken, porridge or cereal served, beds tidied and preparations made for breakfast and the eventual arrival of the day staff. On their arrival at 8.00 a.m. breakfast was issued forth, after which the normal cleaning procedures from the non-nursing staff took over. Late in the morning any visits required from the ward doctor or his consultant took place along with the other mundane activities like X-rays, dressings and bed baths. Next came lunch, which for me was the highlight of the day; come to think of it though, it came and went leaving me wondering why I had been waiting on it from breakfast time. In the afternoons we had what was known as our 'quiet time' when complete relaxation and silence was the rule. Shortly after 4 p.m. in the afternoon we had our evening meal. After this any routine jobs which still required attention from the morning work were completed. Beds were again tidied and everything was seen to be in shipshape and Bristol fashion in readiness for visiting time. Once visiting hour was over, the serving of tea, Horlicks or cocoa heralded the arrival into our lives of the night staff, that gallant body of ladies dedicated to watch over us through the wee small hours. The biggest battle for survival we had to contend with was the sheer boredom of it all. The all too predictable routine of being caught in the daily round of things. The vicious circle of unrelieved monotony beginning from dawn till dusk.

Words could not describe the debt of gratitude owed to those organizations who laid on for us such treats as film shows and concerts, going even to the lengths of putting on for us a complete Dixie Minstrel Show.[12] On evenings such as these rules were wisely waived to one side and our female counterparts shared these social occasions. These events, taking place as they did at times in an atmosphere so recently visited by pain and death, only underlined the fact that one could not afford to become too emotionally involved or feel too deeply, or make each tragedy a personal one for any length of time. To do so would be to court disaster. There had to be a release of tension both for the long-term patient

---

[12] We now accept that these shows portrayed racist stereotypes, but at this time they were viewed purely as entertainment and many audiences were ignorant of the inherent racism.

and the nursing staff. This was a principle of hospital life accepted by patients and nursing staff alike. Patients would still smuggle their radio into the loo, gathering around it to catch the winner of the Grand National or the latest football or cricket match.

Even though the shadow of death hung heavy over the ward, nurses would laugh and joke as they made a bed recently vacated in death by someone they had just nursed. Life had to go on. They could only give so much: to attempt to give more would be suicidal. To take each ward's pain and grief and make it their own would have rendered them emotionally and physically incapable of carrying out their duties. Still, they were creatures of great feeling and a tremendous sense of humour. I learnt to love every one of them.

Though I am sure there were times when we were a great strain on their patience, practical jokes were an almost everyday occurrence, though I must admit it was far from one-way traffic in this respect. The unwary recruit to the nursing profession had to pick her steps carefully if she was not to fall an unwitting victim. I saw one young lady who looked as if she had a great rural tradition behind her fall easy prey to the practical jokers. The ward handbell, which normally heralded an end to visiting time, was the object used in this joke, the young lady being informed that the termination of the rest period was signalled by an enthusiastic ringing of the bell in order to awaken the sleepy heads from their deep slumbers. Sure enough with great eagerness and dexterity, well within the physical capacity of this young lady, she walked up and down among the rows of beds, to use a description of a senior member of staff, playing merry hell. The older and more senile thought it was the signal for some sort of divine retribution, so rudely were they awakened: you know, 'The Bells of Hell Go Ting-a- ling-a-ling'. But more than often the last laugh went to the nursing staff.

I can recall being particularly trying to this night nurse in one way and another, the climax coming one night as she pushed her little trolley around the ward. Out of the kindness of her big heart she had, as an extra treat to our usual nightcap, provided us with a little extra in the form of toast and jam. She was pushing her trolley and radiating all over with deep feelings of great Christian charity. Accepting my usual nightcap of Horlicks I declined any toast and jam. She had crossed the ward when I called out 'Jam!' Thinking I had changed my mind, she descended upon me like a mother hen whose expression tells its own story. 'Jam!' I exclaimed again. She nodded and I responded, 'That's alright, that is what I thought it was, no thank you all the same.'

Later in the evening she came and sat upon my bed.

'Victor, I have just been reading something about you, which has enabled me to be big-hearted and forgive you for what you did this evening.'

'You have!' I exclaimed.

'Yes, and I think we can let bygones be bygones and to prove my good faith I am going to prepare a special treat for you first thing in the morning.'

'You are?' I said.

'Yes,' she replied and smiled, but declined to say what she had been reading about me to bring about this sudden change in attitude, but I was soon to learn.

At 5.50 a.m. I was gently awakened to discover that the screens were encircling my bed. There she stood, a picture of charm itself. 'Do you remember that I promised you a little treat, Victor? Well, just in case it should cause you any embarrassment with your friends I have, as you can see, pulled the screens around us.' She turned to her trolley from which she took a tray covered with a white cloth. Her face beamed all over as she removed the cloth and lifted from the tray a tube at least three feet long. 'Now I am going to get the greatest pleasure and satisfaction from watching and helping you swallow every inch of this.' To emphasize her point she held the tube in both hands, stretching it to its limits, pushing it under my nose as she did so. 'You see Victor, what I had been reading about you was this little detail,' (She gave the tube a twirl in her hands) 'left for you by the sister.' Did you ever try to swallow the contents of a tube first thing in the morning? I am afraid my attempts at swallowing it were anything but private and personal. Soon my mates had taken a lively interest in what was going on to the sadistic delight of the night nurse.

141

Sean, my Good Samaritan, had by this time left us, being transferred to another hospital on the outskirts of Belfast. It was a sad moment for me when we shook hands. Even in parting he attempted to reassure me regarding my own recovery. I knew him for so short a time but his kindness to me when I particularly needed it is one of my life's pleasant memories. Bobby became my new bed neighbour, he was a Christian by profession and a Methodist by choice. He became a practical friend. His deep and rich experience of life was something he willingly shared with me. He was one of those few people who had learnt the fundamentals of human adjustment. He had that rare quality of never allowing himself to be embarrassed by the shortcomings and confidences of others. His smile and personality were his most lethal weapons, making him the easiest person in the world to talk to, though I must confess that I quite often disagreed with his more liberal views on life. Never once as we discussed religion and politics did he ever allow my arrogance born of the foolishness of youth to upset him. More than often the last word on the subject was allowed to rest with me. Sometimes I think his admiration for my enthusiasm allowed him to ignore my zeal, which more than often was not according to knowledge. As an older man I believe he was having a profound influence on me, guiding me to a more mature and satisfactory view of life.

Bryce was a young man and also a new arrival occupying a bed further down the ward and with whom I became very friendly. These two were the chief architects of much of the fun and games that relieved some of the tension and boredom of our lives. I now regarded myself as something of an old hand in the ward having witnessed, mostly from a horizontal position, the passing of three full calendar months. By this time, of course, what with one thing and another, it was well known among the staff that I came from the heart of loyalist Sandy Row. This caused me to be the object of quite a lot of ribbing from some of the nurses. One in particular whose job at that time was to dole out our daily dosage of tablets, on coming to me she would count out the tablets describing them in colourful detail as she did so. Looking at her list she would say 'For Victor we have two green tablets, two white and low and behold two gold! Halibut oil tablets, all to be taken in that order', counting them onto my outstretched hand as she spoke. 'Now get these good Glenavy colours down you and they'll do you the world of good.'

On St. Patrick's morning the sister marched into the ward and stopped with great deliberation at my bed, smiling as she did so in a manner which made it quite clear she was about to involve herself in something which was going to give her a great deal of satisfaction. 'Victor, I have a present for you.' She brought from behind her back a bunch of shamrock which she proceeded to pin onto my pyjamas. 'If you take the shamrocks out or let anything happen to them, I'll fix you my boy, remember, I'll be back to inspect them.'

Shortly afterwards, as good as her word, she came back to examine her precious bunch of shamrocks, which by that time were wilting. Standing back from the bed, hands on her hips, her usual posture when she was about to deliver a lecture she began, 'Sure,' bursting out laughing as she continued on, 'I should have known the poor shamrocks would never have survived in such a hostile environment.'

Chapter 12
Paddy the Goat

About this time Paddy came into our ward, known affectionately among us as Paddy the Goat because of the long tradition he and his father before him had as goat butchers in Belfast. Paddy was an old gentleman to whom the years had endowed with clear and well-defined social habits. One of these was his daily pints, and let me state quite categorically it wasn't milk either. Paddy at such a late stage in life just could not understand or appreciate the hospital not allowing him to bring some of that soothing beverage into the ward. But Paddy, though he did not know it then, was destined to have a visit from a rather unusual doctor who was to appear before him one night in the form of a fairy godfather.

This little farce was to be enacted out by John and Bryce. The stage was set when the day staff had dispersed and we were committed into the dedicated hands of our solitary night nurse. Enter John as the doctor equipped with white coat and stethoscope, accompanied by Bryce in the attire of a male nurse, complete with an old X-ray plate. Both arrived at the bed of the helpless Paddy, stopping at the foot of his bed where they engaged in a momentary discussion over Paddy's chart clipped at the foot of his bed. Moving nearer to Paddy, Bryce took the initiative, 'Doctor,' he addressed himself to John, 'this is Mr Patrick Hynds who was admitted to the ward a little over a week ago and seems to have some difficulty settling down and adjusting himself to hospital life.' John gave a curt nod in Paddy's direction at the same time asking to see Paddy's supposed X-ray 'Could I just have a look at his X-ray?' Holding it up to the light, John gives it a close scrutiny, giving the customary reaction, 'Ah, aha, yes, well,' the cryptic tone seeming to signify something important, but tell you nothing. Then turning to the nurse he enquired, 'No problems with Patrick's normal body functions?' Bryce answered, 'None whatsoever doctor, however Patrick seems unable to settle down and content himself.' All the while as they discussed Paddy, his eyes kept darting from one to the other. John for the first time involved Paddy in the conversation, 'Is this true Mr Hynds? What seems to be the problem?' Paddy, glad of the opportunity to have a sympathetic ear at last, pours out his whole sorry tale describing with great emotion just how unbearable life had become without the succour of a drink to see him through the day, John stood for a moment as though in deep reflection. 'Well, I tell you nurse, I see no reason why Patrick here should not be given two bottles of specially treated Guinness, I think they call it Double X, each day along with his lunch.' Paddy, to say the least, was more than magnanimous in his thanks, calling down the divine blessing upon the doctor's head. 'God bless you, doctor. God bless you, sir.'

The following day saw lunchtime come and go without any sign of the promised beverage. Paddy by this time, was banging his spoon upon his dinner plate (both of which he had refused to give up) to attract attention. No one could pacify him or apparently understand him. At last the ward sister was sent for and Paddy in great detail described how this doctor the night previous had so kindly put him on two bottles of stout per day, guaranteed to arrive promptly with each lunch. The sister questioned him at great length over this mysterious visitation. 'What, for instance, was the doctor's name?' Paddy all the while becoming increasingly impatient retorted, 'I do not know any name, the only name that had come up in their conversation was Guinness and where the hell was it?' Paddy was eventually calmed down with the promise that the whole question of a refreshment for him would be looked into.

Periodically we had a change of day and night staff in the ward, this was always a time fraught with danger for the unwary, both for the patient as well as the nurse. I can recall at the introduction of our new night nurse being set up as easily as you like. With my period of time in the ward now running to four months I was in the happy position, unlike

Bobby and Bryce, of having completed my course of PAS,[13] the most evil and foul-tasting medicine imaginable. Its taste was unbearable, both at the time of swallowing and its reaction later on to the taste buds and the stomach, not to mention the colour it left your teeth. Still, we consoled ourselves in the commonly-held belief, rightly or wrongly, that all the best medicines are the most foul to the taste. A detailed chart was kept on which was recorded the names of those patients who were receiving any form of treatment whatever. Listed against their names were the courses of medicine or injections they were having and the stage reached. A new nurse arriving in a ward without any previous knowledge of her patients was heavily committed to this chart. Our new night nurse arrived in our ward and at a brief glance, and without any introduction formal or informal, we were able to deduce she was a real good-looker with all the necessary qualifications required by an all-in wrestler. She came from Ballymena and there was definitely no mistaking that. My geographical position in the ward, situated at the furthest point away from the recess where all our medicinal concoctions issued forth, meant that I was usually among the last recipients. At the appointed time, our new nurse made her personal appearance with the medicine trolley trundling up the ward, just at the precise moment when Bryce, who lay at the

---

[13] PAS – para-aminosalicylic acid. Primarily used to treat tuberculosis.

other end of the ward from me, decided to attract my attention. Having done this he called up to me in a manner which made me think, he had taken leave of his senses.

'Bryce', he shouted at me, 'I will bring up that book later on.' He was, I recalled referring to a book he had promised to lend me. Poor Bryce I thought he must have finally cracked as he was using his name as if it were mine. Had I but noticed his brief encounter with the new nurse when she asked his name I would have been posing the question when had he acquired mine? Just as she approached my bed Bobby spoke to me calling me Bryce. I thought to myself had everyone gone mad? By this time the night nurse was addressing herself to me, 'And what is your name?' I replied, 'Bryce' to my utter disbelief that I had not given my real name. Bobby at this smiled his usual smile for the occasion, advising me 'Bryce, you had better give her your real name.' The big night nurse had by this time already made up her own mind as to what my correct name was. It was Bryce Martin and I was listed for a full dosage of PAS, which she had decided by hook or by crook I was going to get. I could read her whole approach to the situation. It was her first night on this ward and she was going to put her foot down right from the start, she was not going to let any smart Johnny make a mug of her. Start as you intend to go on was her motto. But I was equally determined that l was not going back onto PAS again, not even for this big blonde bombshell. In the resultant struggle, most of the foul tasting stuff went all over my pyjamas. Certainly, by this time, none of it had gone into my mouth. I must hasten to add that the struggle which ensued with this attractive young lady, taking place as it did across my bed, was not wholly without its compensations. Unwilling to accept defeat, she rallied help around her in the form of Bryce and Bobby. Both apologized afterwards for my predicament, claiming that when this attractive young female asked for their help, their willpower just went to pieces and they could not refuse. Each of them secured an arm while she held my nose, down my throat trickled most of the full dosage, all the while I kept thinking to myself wee apples will grow again.

Chapter 13

The Great Social Leveller

One thing became apparent to me as the months went by – hospital life was a great social leveller. No great social demands or pressures were made upon us. A set of pyjamas and a dressing gown, either one's own or that provided by the hospital, and our attire was complete. A man from the most humble beginnings and with an income to match was able, in a fantasy world of his own making, to see himself hobnobbing with those who, in normal circumstances outside the hospital gates, moved in an entirely different world. I had set myself the task of trying to pin a social label on those different patients whose background I was ignorant of, particularly the few who seemed to be aspiring to be seen as those who moved in a completely different social world from what their meagre circumstances would suggest. I would lie in reflection and try to reconcile the two totally different pictures that often came across of the same person: the one taken during the normal life of the ward and the other, completely irreconcilable to it, taken at visiting time. The analogy which this train of thought often suggested to me was that of a photographic darkroom. I thought of the negative which left plenty of scope for the fertile mind to work on, the dull obscure shadowy figures and surroundings that left themselves open to colourful interpretation. With a little imagination this shadowy world might become clothed in accordance with the inner needs and desires of the moment. What a contrast this was to the developed photograph with its harsh forthright portrayal of life's realities, the beautiful and the ugly, and its sometimes cruel attention to detail.

There was Gerry, who I always thought during his stay in hospital lived in the shadowy world of the unreal, that world almost peculiar to children, the land of make-believe, of once upon a time. I suppose as a mild form of escapism it was a harmless exercise. This was especially noticeable in his dealings with Mr Simpson who was a gentleman of obvious class and distinction. In communicating with him Gerry's whole personality underwent a complete transformation. His speech acquired what I would refer to as an upper Malone income bracket, where good grammar is secondary to correct pronunciation of such words as jug, butcher and vase. He was usually at his best when he and Mr Simpson attempted to lose themselves in the rapture of Dvorak's 'New World Symphony' or some other piece which they frequently listened to on the third radio programme, both of them lying on the top of their respective beds baring their souls as they prostrated themselves before the masters. Mr Simpson would often enquire of Gerry if he could detect the dominant instrument coming through on each stanza. Gerry, I must admit, was never lost for an answer and probably had a sound secondary knowledge of the classics. If he had only tried less to appear to be clever. On one such occasion, which springs to mind quite readily, Mr Simpson, in a rather perplexed mood, enquired of Gerry if he thought the French horn was coming though with more power and feeling than the part demanded. Gerry began as he usually did with his overuse of the word actually,. 'Actually, Ronald,' (he was now on first name terms with Mr Simpson) 'I rather thought the French horn actually submerged quite gradually and naturally with the actual background music.' Lying in bed as I was, daydreaming, the whole topic of their conversation barely bordering on the field of my subconsciousness set my imagination working overtime as I began to see the French horn player and the complete orchestra – how was it Gerry had put it? – 'Sink quite gradually and naturally' below the ocean, in much the same fashion as the dance band in the film of the *Titanic* made their exit beneath the waves playing, very appropriately, 'Nearer My God To Thee'. (I personally was a philistine in relation to classical music, regarding the musical film *Rose Marie*, starring Nelson Eddy and Jeanette MacDonald, as the ultimate in high-brow stuff. As far as being able to recognize the sound of a French horn, I admit

153

the only horn I was ever conscious of identifying was that of Blythe Street Mill as it summoned the workers from Sandy Row and beyond to its gruesome construction, a nineteenth-century giant in the twentieth century.) That was the negative of Gerry, but the actual photograph was quite different, and was best seen at visiting time when Gerry, having more in common with the proletariat crowd, identified with Maximilien Robespierre and the French Revolution. Poor Gerry. When the time came for him to leave us, we gave him a farewell like a long tone from a French horn. Stripped of the hospital attire in which he felt in his own world and a common identity with such men as Mr Simpson, he now looked a pathetic creature as he proceeded down the ward, only stopping to bid farewell and shake hands with the great man. His baggy trousers were shiny and well worn, his coat was quite different in colour and style from his trousers and looked as if it had once belonged to a man a lot less his size. His hastily bundled brown paper parcel, in which was contained his worldly goods (they all told their own story) gave the lie to the Gerry he at times projected upon us in his moments of fantasy. I felt sorry for him as eyes other than mine watched him depart. The words came to me, 'To thine own self be true'. If Gerry had not put up such a pretence, then he probably would have left our ward a taller man in stature even than the gentleman he so ardently attempted to impress. But Gerry's momentary flights into the world of make-believe were child's play in comparison to the fantasy world lived in by John Bridges.

John was admitted to our ward close on the departure of Gerry. He was a man of stocky build and average height, and probably middle-aged. His weather-beaten and tanned complexion almost matching in colour his more than generous mop of straight brown hair, which more often than not hung over his forehead, and that, with his deep-set eyes and high cheek bones gave him an almost ape-like appearance. The solitary earring which hung from his left ear further added to the suggestion, borne out by his complexion, that he was a man of the open air, a Gypsy by birth, a tinker by profession. He made me think of some of the Gypsy characters portrayed by Jefferey Farnol in *Peregrine's Progress*. John was no ordinary Gypsy, as I was soon to learn. Now in my fifth month I was in the privileged position of being allowed up in the evening for a short spell. Those of us who enjoyed this privilege usually gathered around the small open fire in the ward for a chit-chat over our nightly bedtime beverage. John's medical history had yet to be sorted out and as a temporary arrangement he was allowed up for toilet facilities and a brief period in the evening. On this spring evening, as we chatted over our Horlicks and cocoa, John and I were left alone, the rest having retired for the night. John in a very deliberate action pulled his chair closer to mine and at the same time, rather strangely, glanced furtively around him in an attempt to make sure no one was listening. Then began the most amazing tale that I in my relatively short experience of life encountered. John, who was normally slow to enter into our conversation, set about his subject with great gusto. He had been in hospital across the water when, for reasons which he had still to reveal to me, he had been warned of an attempt to be made on his life. This was to take place under the guise of a stomach operation, the doctor having diagnosed John as suffering from an active stomach ulcer that required surgery. But John knew better. The doctor was a paid hireling of those who sought to terminate his life. The whole thing was a cunning plot to end his life in the operating theatre. Under such conditions a hundred and one reasons could be given for his demise. John, forewarned about this plot on his life, had done the obvious thing and absconded before it was too late. But they refused to be beaten, following him relentlessly throughout the length and breadth of England, finally running him to ground in the port of Liverpool. Here they eventually had him certified as insane and accordingly institutionalized. These were the blackest days of John's whole existence, for having him safely locked away they could in their cold and clinical way prepare to move towards a final solution to the problem of John Bridges. All the while he spoke, his eyes watching me intently, I had the feeling that in his own way he was interpreting the slightest reaction on my part. Up to this point I had no idea who had warned him of his impending doom, or why such a highly organized attempt, obviously coming as it did from those with a great deal of authority, should be directed against the life of this simple Gypsy. What was so unique about him to attract such attention, and what cloak and dagger intrigue had he allowed himself to become involved in? Moving closer, John went through the motions of ascertaining that we were again unheard as he related his escape from the institution. Suddenly, on the approach of the night nurse, he grabbed my arm. I rightly interpreted it as a signal for us to be on our guard until she had passed. He continued on, now almost in a whisper. His whole being now appeared to be shocked through and through with deep emotional feeling, his grip on my arm tightening as, barely audible, he whispered in my ears, 'You see I am a direct heir to the throne of England.' It is at moments like these that a writer usually claims there was a 'pregnant pause'. Pause there was, but I struggled to hide my true feelings, realizing that I was now listening to the ravings of an insane man and, who having revealed the dramatic secret of his noble birth, watched intently for an intelligent and sympathetic response from me. I am afraid the best I could come up with in the circumstances was 'Is that so?' John continued, 'But just how close in line, I am not at all sure yet, but mark you this, they will not cheat John Bridges out of his royal inheritance.' I was rescued with the raising of the alarm signalling the approach of the night sister.

Poor John's kingdom in a real sense, was not of this world, but one which existed only in his deranged mind, the figment of his own imagination. A few days later John had to be forcibly removed from the ward and sent to a specialized part of the hospital especially prepared for those who have lost touch with reality. John's departure from our ward caused quite a bit of excitement, the big doctor who was a rugby player of some repute having to struggle with him before he was able to give him the injection that left him temporarily paralysed from the waist down, enabling them to remove him quite easily despite John's pathetic pleas. For John the vicious circle begun across the water was turning full circle again.

Chapter 14

Admitted to a Sanatorium

A few short weeks after John had gone, it was my turn to leave the ward. I can assure you I put up no struggle although I suppose to a certain extent my exit was no less dramatic. I had spent six full calendar months of my life in this small ward; now I was more than glad to leave. My friends gave me a party the night before I left. I will always treasure the happy memories we shared, borne out of life's adversities. The sister made me promise that I should have my clothes sent up the day before I left. She said failure to do so would only delay indefinitely my departure from the ward. A suitcase containing my clothes arrived accordingly, the day before my departure. That night I guarded it with great care, but when sleep overtook me, my suitcase vanished. I had my interview with the doctor the morning of my departure and was given the green light to go home. But to where? I had no clothes! Sister passed me still in bed. With a twinkle in her eye she exclaimed, 'What! not away home yet Victor? Perhaps you will stay for lunch.' I was not interested in lunch but how quickly I could get out and home. My clothes eventually turned up and I rushed into my trousers, and in the process my feet refused to go down through the legs. The bottoms had been sewn, preventing my feet to go through. Someone had gone to a lot of trouble, even the very buttonholes of my spare were sewed. It was a sort of ritual which I saw as a recognition on their part of my impending departure, and to which they were giving an air of finality. But it was all a little premature. I had barely time to adjust myself to life outside, stripped of the restrictions imposed upon me as a patient, when after my first attendance at the Durham Street Clinic I was put on a further course of PAS. Thus, I became an outpatient attending the clinic consuming two sachets of PAS five times daily in the process. The signs for me were ominous.

One Saturday morning at the end of January a letter arrived at No. 12 addressed to me. On opening it I discovered it was thought necessary for me to be admitted for further medical treatment. I felt this time life was taking the form of an operation. My father read the letter and he predictably told me to forget about it. 'You have gone through enough,' he said. It was a big temptation for me to agree, but if the hospital had taught me anything, it was this: that it would not be in my best interests not ignore the hospital advice. My father was talking with his heart and not his head. So just over eight months since I was discharged from hospital,

I was to be admitted to a sanatorium in the suburbs of Belfast, with the promise that something more definite would be attempted this time.

In February I was admitted to hospital. My lung was surgically collapsed and artificially maintained in this condition for another three years. After an initial six months' hospitalization I was discharged, attending for the remainder of the time at the Clinic for weekly refills.

I quickly settled down to hospital life again, having made up my mind once more, by a process of adoption and cooperation, to make my stay as short as medically possible. In comparison with my former abode I was soon to learn that there were considerable differences in the routine of this new hospital. Visiting time in the former being spread over every day in the week was now confined to Wednesday, Saturday and Sunday only. This was something which I accepted quite readily, realizing it would make less demands upon my parents and friends, my parents in particular having insisted on visiting me at every opportunity which availed itself.

One obvious change was that of structural design. Where previously I had been hospitalized in a conventional brick building, this was nothing more or less than a prefabricated Nissen hut. The sanatorium itself was no more than a collection of these huts, each one facing the other. A solid brick corridor connected the huts to the main hospital and was the main artery connecting one set of Nissen huts to another, as they ran parallel with each other along the whole length of the corridor, about twenty in all. What I regarded as the top half was furthest away from the main building and housed the men. The bottom half nearest the main general hospital was for the women. In the area of the corridor occupied by the women was the tuck shop and chapel. The whole complex reminded one of a miniature village, except the analogy of a village could not be maintained with the obvious segregation of the sexes and the absence of any organized social functions like those we enjoyed at my previous hospital. Here they were almost non-existent. In fact, I cannot recall one social activity during my whole six months' stay. There was of course no television in the wards in those days and, what with the visiting confined to the three afternoons, the evenings were fraught with boredom.

Another thing which depressed me on arrival was the realization that most patients (those that did not discharge themselves) could look forward on average to a lengthy stay in hospital, anything in fact from a year upwards. Many I knew personally had already been there longer than two years. The ward into which I was admitted treated not only those whose afflictions attacked their lungs but also a small number of patients, about six in all, whose ailments were confined to their spine and, in some cases, the joints of the knee. It was the courage of some of these patients which helped me to quickly adjust to my new surroundings and conform to whatever small inconveniences hospital life had to offer. To be restricted to bed apart from for the use of the normal toilet facilities was no hardship when one realized the conditions under which patients like Jimmy were confined.

Jimmy was a young married man, a tradesman in the shipyard, suffering from a diseased area of the spine, who was literally encased from head to toe in plaster, so he looked like an Egyptian mummy. When I first met Jimmy he had already been well over a year lying under such conditions, but I am glad to say, such is the indestructible human spirit, before I left he had just about made his first few faltering steps around the bottom of his bed, well on the way to recovery. It was a great moment for all of us to hear his howls of laughter echo throughout the ward as the young nurses set about him, giving him a bed bath, and his promise of retaliation should he ever get out of this coffin set me to thinking that surely this is the unbridgeable gap between us and the highest form of animal life, the ability to accept the future with all its promises of pain and frustration and yet live each day at a time. Conscious of our own strength and determination to face the inevitable with the knowledge that 'hope springs Eternal' only in the human breast, as I lay there thinking of Jimmy, as his laughter echoed throughout the ward giving a promise of hope and a new day for all of us, I couldn't but help think of the words from a poem by Robert Burns who, whilst ploughing on a November day, ruined the nest of a field mouse. Burns ponders why the creature runs away in such terror.

Still thou art blessed, compared with me!
The present only touches thee,
But, oh, I backward cast my eye
On prospects drear,
I guess and fear.[14]

Surely here, amidst the smell of antiseptics and liquid ether, was the ideal setting for separation, the mice from the men or vice versa.

There may have been no television but we still had our earphones. They were comfort to us during the long evenings. It was quite an experience, really, to switch off and listen to the reaction the *Goon Show* received as each patient in turn responded to whatever joke or comical situation tickled his fancy the most. Imagine the ward, deadly quiet with no audible communication whatsoever, everyone intently listening in. Suddenly the silence is broken by sporadic bursts of individual laughter, sometimes in unison, at other times one burst following upon another. To anyone not conscious of what was happening it must have appeared that we were under the influence of laughing gas or else had cracked up altogether, every one of us, to a man.

For some, of course, there were unnatural strains put upon them brought about by the obvious celibacy imposed on those who would not otherwise have been so committed. To counteract this we were often told that bromide had been

---

14 Taken from 'To a Mouse' by Robert Burns

put in our tea. Whether this was so or not I had no knowledge except to say if true, then its failure rate was quite high. Though we had a male doctor in charge of our ward I can recall the occasion when we had a lady doctor committed to our ward for a few days in the absence of our own doctor. This young lady had what could only be described as a very ample bosom. It had been rumoured that never once had she been able to get an acceptable blood pressure reading from a patient. This I could easily believe. Sammy who lay opposite to me, on hearing of her physical form, decided he required the services of this temporary ward doctor of ours for a pain that he had suddenly developed low down in the abdomen. Sure enough as expected she entered the ward to the admiration of all her virile and hot-blooded admirers, all anxious to catch a glimpse of her bedside manner. Her white coat was flying wide open revealing her low cut dress, even lower than usual and having even less control and restrictions upon her bosom, which was particularity noticeable as she jogged over the floor, in her high-heeled shoes, towards Sammy's bed. She bent over Sammy and she prodded around his abdomen in order to get the correct response that would indicate the affected area. As I watched his performance I realized his weakness (which was quite natural under the circumstances) lay in his oohs and aahs. They were quite good, but as time went on the proper facial expression which should have been coordinated with the painful response was missing. Instead he beamed all over with deep satisfaction and rather obvious enjoyment, which was hardly the correct facial expression expected of someone who had a firm hand pressed upon their tender spot, even if it did belong to a pretty female showing much of her cleavage to full view. With complete dedication and a no-nonsense technique, she brought the examination to a sudden conclusion. With an abruptness that surprised everyone, she gave Sammy a hefty smack across the jaw before storming out of the ward amidst the howls of hysterical laughter of the onlookers.

Our ward sister was a quiet person who performed her duties accordingly, but none the less effectively for all that. She was known affectionately among us as Mamsie. She had a familiar stock-in-trade expression when faced with any misdemeanour that echoed her undaunted faith in human nature. She would often say, 'Why, I would never at all thought it possible of you. I must say I am greatly surprised.' Her outward approach to her patients appeared to be one of reserve and non-involvement, but behind that cool exterior, we were in no doubt, beat a heart of gold and we respected her all the more for it. She was also a Roman Catholic, as indeed was our ward doctor, thus hands across the divide were still reaching out to me, including my friendship with Bobby Bonnar, brother of the more famous Paddy whom I had often watched as a boy when Celtic played the Blues. The long clear nights of summer were upon us, the cold days of winter now but a bleak memory.

Chapter 15

My Progress Went in Leaps and Bounds

Quite often into our ward came some of those well-meaning gentlemen wearing their collars turned back to front. More often than not the approach of some of them to sickness left a lot to be desired. Their gospel of gloom and despondency was more geared to frustrate the inhabitants than regenerate. One of these reverend gentlemen was well known among us for his off-the-cuff quips, none of which I am afraid endeared him to any of us. Sometimes he would appear to cast doubt upon the seriousness of our illness as with a cough and a thump on the chest he would remark 'I wish I looked and felt as well as some of you fellows.' At other times he would enquire, 'What are you doing here?', which particularly annoyed me. I can recall him asking Big Noel, as he made his way awkwardly from his bed in the direction of the loo, 'And what's a big hefty fellow like you doing in here?' Something within me said, 'Shut your blasphemous mouth.' Big Noel lay in the bed next to me and was encased in a plaster which surrounded his waist like a huge corset. A typical gesture of the same gentleman was to invite us to exchange places with him and then, with a smirk and a clean pair of heels, he was off. We noticed he never made it a divine invocation. Another reverend gentleman was notorious for insisting before he left his visitor of saying a short prayer at the bedside; this was used as an excuse and it took the form of a sermon that he preached to the whole ward. His specially acquired pulpit voice rang out harshly and monotonously around the ward as it rose and fell in pitch. The whole discourse was particularly rehearsed for our benefit as he continually related sickness, and a pointed mention of our affliction, to the divine will. This was something I could never understand coming from a supposedly intelligent human being. The most theologically ignorant could not be blamed for wondering if this, as the reverend gentleman said, was so – how some of our most dedicated staff, from both sides of the religious divide who looked upon their calling as having the divine blessing, could be working twenty-four hours a day in order to nurse us back to health and strength and at the same time be at variance with the divine will. Mercifully, those who wore the cloth weren't all the same. Our padre was a solemn bloke, we called him dismal Jim.

This was the restless time when men became conscious of the new world bursting into activity outside, and the urge to be up and away was at its strongest. Sometimes on a summer's evening a bird would fly through an open window in our ward and in its hopeless plight a parable unfolded itself. The poor creature momentarily trapped most often found a means of escape through another window. Others were not so lucky. Often in a frantic attempt to escape the bird would rise as high as the roof permitted then would come the moment of decision as it saw a patch of light, a glimpse of sky, a window of escape. Suddenly, with great deliberation, like a stone falling out of the air, the bird would head straight for a window. The resulting thud as bird flesh met with unyielding glass on impact was saddening. Outside, towering in the background, rose Divis Mountain. The tall trees and rolling fields of the park outside seemed but an arm's length away and reached all the wide expanse of blue and white above. The sky was the limit and freedom lay as far as the eye could see, yet here, in this minute speck of a hut, the poor bird had trapped herself. Now crumpled and cold, a moment of inquisitiveness and recklessness meant life was gone. It all seemed so senseless, the bird was a creature of flight, freedom belonged to the bird, it was its birth right. To die this way was a mockery of nature's scheme of things. To fall in the ceaseless struggle for survival would be nature's way, but to be imprisoned in a dingy hut surrounded by an ocean of sky was not what nature intended.

After my operation my progress went in leaps and bounds and I was now in the position of being permitted up in the afternoons for a few hours. During this time I was allowed to dress and walk around the grounds or, if visiting time, go with my visitors for a walk in the park. This (at first) was an embarrassing time for me as I had been corresponding with a young lady from the bottom wards in which lay our female counterparts. We corresponded through the media known in hospital as pigeon post, the actual pigeon in most cases being our staff nurse. Now that I was on my feet for a few hours it was expected by one and all that I would pay the young lady a visit, but I felt at the time that this would not be in our best interests, so the correspondence stopped and, despite what our staff nurse thought to the contrary, I gave the female ward a wide berth.

As the only patient in our ward allowed up it was expected that I should go to the tuck shop in the evening on behalf of the patients in our ward. For some reason it gave Mamsie a great deal of satisfaction to see me take my job so seriously. Equipped with a notebook and pencil I made my round of our ward and the ward directly opposite, which had no one to fulfil this duty for them. Seeing me make the rounds she would say with unconcealed enthusiasm, 'Good evening Victor, off to the shop for the boys?' I had the feeling she felt I was carrying out a small errand of mercy that was good for morale and something which she deeply appreciated. Alex, who lay on the bed next to mine, decided to take what he thought was a handout from me on my first journey to the tuck shop by adding to his list of requests Eau De Cologne Bath Salts, but the laugh was on him when I arrived back with a full packet which I handed over to him to the accompanying catcalls and whistles from the boys in the ward.

We were now well into the 'mad month' and the fact that the Field was only a few acres away meant that when the glorious day came and the sound of fife and drum ascended to the heavens adorned in an Orange halo, caught in the breeze and wafted to the four corners, then it was only natural that some of it should reach us, picked up by the ultra-sensitive hearing specially acquired by all Orangemen on this, their day, the 12th J^uly. Paddy strained and listened. He was a countryman with many an evening behind him when he had sat with his dog listening for the slightest sound that would tell him they were still hot on the scent of their prey, but on this particular day I believe he pretended he could hear nothing. But there the sound was again, surely Paddy could hear that! Now and then music from the bands wafted into the air, distorted by distance till it resembled the sadistic rhythm of some far-off jungle tom-tom drums. But nevertheless its message was clear and distinct above all else. The boys had arrived, our blood was up. Paddy laughed, shook his head and agreed we were all mad. To some who were allowed up the nearness of the field where it was all happening was too great a temptation so they attempted the journey across the fields. Harry from Sandy Row, with blue blood in his veins, boasted he had never missed a Twelfth yet and by all that was Orange and Purple he wasn't going to miss one now. So he joined the select few whose enthusiasm failed to take into account the effects upon their fitness of a long sojourn in hospital. King William crossed the Boyne but Harry had to contend with an open ditch on his way to the celebrations. Unfortunately his long confinement put obvious restrictions upon his agility and he ended up in the ditch soaked to the skin. Someone rather unkindly remarked, 'At least he didn't have a dry Twelfth anyway.'

It was decided in our ward that we should in some way identify ourselves with our brethren in their celebrations, and so was born probably one of the first ecumenical lodge gatherings. Paddy contributed his crutches as fine poles for the banner, which consisted of a blue counterpane from one of the beds, into which was stuck a photo of the Queen. Thus our banner was complete. Hughie brought along his accordion and, believe it or not, from somewhere someone even produced a drum. We made a short tour of both wards and finally grouped together for our photograph to be taken, Paddy doing us the honour of helping to carry the banner. We were, all told, a rather mixed bunch from across the divide, but we shared a common awareness, that which comes to those who had to watch a large piece of their world go by from a horizontal position: an acute realization of having one's priorities right. After all, give a man a choice as to whether he would rather be a sick Orangeman or Hibernian than a healthy non-participant, then I know what he would plump for any day.

Chapter 16

So Smile When You're in Trouble, it Will Vanish Like A Bubble

Shortly after the Twelfth, into our ward arrived old Alex, kicking up a racket of his own volition, but most certainly not under his own steam as he was carried on a stretcher and deposited into a bed almost directly opposite my own. To all intents and purposes he seemed, at first glance, to be a typical old gentleman, rather frailer than most, but no less dignified-looking in his twilight years. His most prominent feature was a hook-like nose, which seemed to be specially designed to hold up the biggest pair of spectacles I had ever seen on such a small man. His snow-white hair circled no further upwards than the tips of his ears. A closer look at Alex and it did not take Sherlock Holmes to deduce, by the colour of his bald head, that Alex had led a very active outdoor life, even up to quite recently. Here was no old gentleman tucked away in some old people's home or some relative's parlour to be brought out for his final demise. Here was an old man who apparently had lived life to the full prior to his admission and, as we were later to discover, done his own thing. Alex's one obvious physical defect, quite natural for his years, was his hearing, which he sought to correct by cupping his hands to his ears in trumpet-like fashion. This failing had the effect of gifting him with a voice which sounded as if it had found its way through one of those old fashioned trumpet-type speakers once used at open-air meetings. But one thing I think the years had omitted to teach Alex was to grow old gracefully. His attitude to the nursing staff, to put it mildly, left a lot to be desired. From Alex's arrival in our ward, his constant bone of contention between him and the nurses was the position of his mattress. This, in common with many others in the ward, was a result of him being small. He constantly slid down to the bottom of his bed. Despite being given extra pillows, the constant shifting of the mattress only lowered his position in the bed and led to a continual round of hostilities. The commencement of these was usually heralded by Alex eventually managing somehow to struggle his top half into a somewhat vertical position and then, with monotonous regularity, yelling out at the top of his voice, 'The mattress, the mattress.' To a new nurse in the ward, previously uninvolved with Alex, his harsh voice and the peculiar way he broke up his syllables made it difficult to understand and locate the cause of all the excitement, particularly when he never entered into any discussion on the matter, but simply kept repeating over and over again, 'The mattress, the mattress.' Poor Alex. His evident hostility to anyone wearing a uniform only made life that little bit more uncomfortable, both for himself and the nursing staff in general. He was, I suppose, the classic example of the difficult patient. Nothing seemed to please him and rarely did he ever smile. His face quite readily adopted an aggressive expression. His whole attitude took the form of a type of psychological warfare waged against the nurses, calling as he did on his undoubted experience and the tough life he had lived to enable him to detect the enemy's weakest point or the slightest flaw in their personality. Any nurse who allowed herself to become involved with him for any great length of time ran the risk of incurring his displeasure and at the same time having any weakness in her make-up exposed. Some persisted in their efforts to try and bring Alex closer to their idea of the ideal patient; all were doomed to failure, as Alex just refused to cooperate.

A certain member of the day staff took it upon herself as her second calling in life to succeed where others had failed, believing that as they shared a common love for anything Scottish this would provide her with a lever to prise open his defensive armour. Alex claimed to have spent forty years of his life in the Highlands. The Scottish accent of the new nurse gave her an obvious identity with Scotland. Her accent appeared to be doing the trick and it looked like definite progress was about to be made as Alex, with unheard of consideration, waited till she appeared before he drew attention to his particular need of the moment, and with such courtesy even a hint of a stifled laugh almost escaped during the proceedings. But alas it was a mistake on her part to see it as a victory. She was asking for too much, too soon. She attempted to make him aware that the world did not end at the bottom of his bed and nurses were not just robots but human beings with pulses and feelings like everyone else. She tried to involve him more in his surroundings and less in himself. It was all so admirable and the ethics sound, but the timing was poor and the method of approach, even taking into account its sincerity, was bound for disaster. The nurse decided to take the apparent progress to a further stage by asking Alex to say hello to everyone, 'Alex, say a big hello to everyone.' There was no response. Just then, Hughie happened to be leaving the bathroom and as he was passing, the nurse asked Alex to introduce himself to Hughie. The silence was deafening as Alex chose to ignore Hughie altogether. In fact, the whole thing seemed to be having the effect you would expect if you had suddenly introduced sugar rationing in a sweetie factory or a bacon sandwich at a Jewish wedding. But if that introduction lacked a certain finesse, worse was to follow as she continued on, 'Ah, come on Alex give us all a big smile, come on son let's all see them toothy pegs.' The danger signals were by this time obvious to me. All this patter had been tried before and one thing Alex disliked was to be patronized or to be treated as a senile old man entering his second childhood. She continued on in her efforts by breaking into a boisterous rendering of:

> It isn't any trouble just to S-M-I-L-E,
> It isn't any trouble just to S-M-I-L-E,
> So smile when you're in trouble,
> It will vanish like a bubble,
> If you'll only take the trouble
> Just to S-M-I-L-E.[15]

The nurse did not notice what effect her solo effort was having on Alex. He was literally bursting with indignation which resulted in him shouting, 'Shut your mouth ye Haggis, Scotch!, Scotch!, you Scotch!, you're no more Scotch than…' He was momentarily lost for words, so great was his anger. Then he continued yelling, 'Scotch!, you're an imposter. Six years in Scotland? I was longer on the Bangor boat.' Alex did not let up on his verbal attack on the nurse and as he pointed his finger directly at her, he shouted, 'That one comes from Portadown, that big haggis would come back talking Scotch after a one-day excursion ticket.' Suddenly he invited everyone to look at him, not that he needed any encouragement, so great was the racket he was

---

[15] 'S-M-I-L-E', children's song, writer unknown. The chapter title is also a quote from this song.

kicking up. 'Look at me. Forty years travelling all over the Highlands and I have never lost the accent of my place of birth yet.' Then he addressed himself to her again, 'Haggis, come over here!' Hesitantly, she approached his bed, unable to make up her mind whether to respond to this rude and abrupt invitation. The discourse which followed was lost on us as it proceeded forth from Alex in a whisper. She turned from the bed and was emotionally upset by whatever remark he had made. She bravely attempted to stifle back the tears that quickly filled her eyes, hurrying from the ward as she did so. Alex, meanwhile, took no further interest in the whole proceedings and lapsed into his usual unapproachable self. Meanwhile, mystery surrounded the details concerning our valiant nurse's sudden departure. That Alex was the culprit went without saying, and some form of verbal abuse the means used, but the subject matter no one knew. Both participants seemed to have disengaged from any further conversation for the moment. Alex to be his own sullen self, while our new nurse had momentarily disappeared from the scene. When she did appear her bloodshot eyes told their own story, but her general countenance seemed to imply that she had wisely put the whole episode behind her as she made her entry into the ward, even managing a smile as she did so. When she had time to think about it, she had realized how unwise it was of her, as a new nurse, to have 'rushed in where angels fear to tread'. Alex remained unconquered, but events were to take a most unusual twist that would catch up with him.

The iceberg was about to feel upon it the warm blasts of the ward's indignation and a definite thaw was about to take place in the process. Notice had been taken of Alex's rather peculiar and disgusting habit around his use of his urine bottle and which was further accentuated by his utter disregard in this matter during visiting time. Alex, for reasons best known to himself, appeared obsessed with the results achieved from his use of the bottle. This he would take from under the bedclothes holding it up high, his face distorted so intently as he scrutinized its contents. His actions were reminiscent of some scientist locked away in his laboratory, hovering on the threshold of identifying some lethal virus to which the world, caught in its deadly grip, waited to hear the outcome with baited breath. But what was Alex looking for with his latest escapade? With the new nurse in mind there were those who suggested it was a shame that the old boy should be disappointed in his mysterious quest. Events moved quickly and a certain individual was seen to fetch a new urine bottle for Alex and deposit it in the receptacle especially fitted to his bed for that purpose. Sure enough, at the appointed time, decreed by nature, the bizarre ritual enacted itself while, to follow the previous illustration, the whole ward waited, hushed in expectancy, conscious that we were about to be spectators to a nerve-shattering discovery.

The moment when it came certainly lived up to all expectations. Suddenly the most unmerciful yell pierced the ward followed by tortured appeals that seemed to rise straight from the very depths of the soul, alternating one after the other, 'Nurse, doctor, nurse, doctor.' So it continued until help appeared on hand in the form of a rather surprised and timorous nurse. Alex by this time was speechless, he just kept gesturing, pointing with one hand to the bottle. No deed or word seemed to pacify him, then, in a moment of sanity, it was realized he had discovered a worm floating about in the contents of the bottle. At this stage he was quite convinced that he had passed it. The doctor was sent for and Alex was eventually made to accept that the worm must have already been in the bottle prior to its use. All this was too much for some of the spectators of this little drama who were by now rolling in their beds with laughter. Alex was in no doubt that it had arrived in the bottle by design and not by accident as he screamed at one and cursed at all around him. Following the latest incident in which he was involved, even Alex came to realize that he was only making life extremely difficult for himself. So it was no surprise when he showed definite signs of thawing out.

Alex received many visits from different organizations who were interested in his eternal welfare. 'Twits' is how he described them. However, he had a different impression of an elderly lady who visited him every Saturday afternoon, bringing him a parcel containing home-baked wheaten bread and a gospel tract for his attention. She impressed him more than all the others and he would often remark about the elderly lady that she is a real Christian.

It was after one such visit from the elderly lady that Alex called me over. 'Open that' he said, pointing to the parcel, 'Now take one.' I felt to decline would have offended him. 'Sit down a minute.' He pointed to the edge of his bed. Next he began to fumble in his locker from which he brought out a bundle of papers and, setting them on top of his bed, he proceeded to give me a brief outline to the story of his life. Long before the catchphrase 'doing your own thing' became popularized, Alex had been doing just that, all over Scotland, refusing to stay in any one place long enough to conform to what could be described as normal living. Wherever he went he described his travels in the form of poetry, evidence which was clearly seen in the pile of papers sitting on top of his bed. In one particular episode in his life, circumstances deemed that he spent the night sleeping rough. He had been well into the highlands and heading for the nearest town when darkness fell and travelling became difficult. To use his own words he selected his spot and got his head down. Tired he slept well into the Sabbath morning, waking to discover he had bedded down in a church graveyard. The sun was shining, the birds were singing and breaking into verse. Alex continued on talking and moved closer to me as he did so, perhaps to further emphasize what he was about to relate.

Church bells were ringing
Calling the faithful onto prayer
But I, an unbeliever,
Neither heed nor care.

It was, I suppose the story of old Alex's life – his failure to conform in the secular world did not stop short of the sacred either. Shortly after Alex's death I was discharged, having spent just over six months in hospital.

Chapter 17
Come On Who'll Be Next?

Now looking better and feeling fitter than I had for a long time, the only apparent connection with my illness was an obvious one: I had to attend for refills once a week for another three years. I also had a scar on my left lung, a permanent legacy of my former illness. The scar was something to be expected, but I was to face the unexpected due to my medical history. It was to have an effect on my personality both following my discharge and later when I was to seek employment. It left me with serious problems. The hospital had healed my body, but it had left grave problems relating to my mental attitude towards my illness. I suppose there are limits to the National Health Service treatments. I was never an extrovert but I became even more introverted. I left hospital feeling different, and I suppose I was different having been the victim of a contagious killer disease to which many had succumbed and I had survived. The nature of my illness had always made me acutely aware of my responsibility to society at large to seek treatment and hospitalization, even when I was discharged. I was conscious of a personal obligation to my family, committing myself to a policy of segregation until my cure was well established, keeping very strictly to my own toilet requisites and culinary utensils. This extended to affecting my relations with others outside my family. I had an abnormal fear of being thought of and seen as one of them suffering from 'it' and therefore a possible hazard to the community's health. It was as if I felt that some stigma was attached to me. It was because of this that I adopted a low profile at any social functions at which I was involved, keeping clear of such menial tasks as pouring out the tea or handling any food. All this had the effect of putting severe restrictions on my personality, making me decidedly inhibited in my personal relationships. It was a defect which I had to work on extremely hard in order to overcome it. Once I was given the all-clear to seek a job I found my medical history put severe restrictions on my ability to gain suitable employment. In the winter of 1954, now three years since I left work due to illness, I was given the green light to seek employment. In order to enable me to find the right sort of job it was decided that I register as an R.D.P. (Registered Disabled Person), entitling me to carry a blue card. This, I was assured, would guarantee me getting the proper sort of job for someone with my medical history. This was to prove a fallacy, if ever there was one.

Now with the dubious honour of holding a blue card, I was sent to a rehabilitation centre at Whitehouse for a course in sheet metal work, lasting two months. There were about a dozen of us at the sheet metal course and a rather mixed bunch at that. Some I recognized from their attendance at the clinic for refills, others had handicaps more obvious. Some, as we were to learn, suffered from disabilities undetectable either to the naked eye or the magic all-revealing eye of the X-ray machine, but no less real and crippling for all that. But we had one depressing thing in common: we were all almost unemployable. One thing was certain, we were no threat to the sheet metal industry, as was witnessed by our instructor's free and easy attitude; he quite clearly did not expect us to set any records. Those of us sufficiently interested in making the effort were encouraged to make various utensils which we were able to purchase for the cost of the material. As it was a few months until Christmas, I set about making a large doll's house for my sister.

Our sheet metal activities were located in a bungalow type building, much the same size as the Nissen hut I had been hospitalized in, but differing in shape and layout, being rectangular and more modern in structure and design, boasting quite a number of fairly large metal-framed windows that opened into two parts as required, giving the whole building a rather bright and comfortable atmosphere, even in those dull days of late autumn. Benches upon which were fastened vices ran along the full length of the walls. The main floor area was given over to simple machinery consisting of a guillotine, a machine for folding and pressing the sheet metal and a single anvil which, like the welding equipment, was situated near the one and only door in use, which was both the entrance and exit.

Among us was a man called Will, who stood out head and shoulders above everyone else, his bull neck and massive body, spread as it was over his huge frame, clearly indicting tremendous physical potential, which appeared totally out of place among us. His verbal communication was generally limited to nods and grunts, leaving his presence in our midst open to much conjecture. This passed from speculation to comments about his quiet disposition and this, measured against the size of the man, was inevitably taken as a sign of weakness. Well, to all intents and purposes, he decided, he needed a friend and so this quiet giant eventually shared his tea breaks with me. Apparently Will, as is typical of many big men, when faced with a situation requiring qualifications and an approach other than those confined to brawn and physical effort, would go to pieces. His married life had been one domestic crisis after another. His wife had left him, unable to cope. Will faced the daily round and demands of life only with the help of his daily dosage of tranquillizers. To emphasize to me the tremendous tension and pressure he was under, he would often thump the side of his head with the palm of his huge hand. Meanwhile, there were those who decided to exploit the quiet, almost docile, big man. His creative efforts were often the subject of open discussion and criticism, the participants unaware that they were trifling with an emotional time bomb. I don't know how many times Will had counted up to ten, but it was evident as the following incident will relate.

Will had decided mathematics were not the answer to his more immediate problems and responded in the only way he knew how. Watching him bend and hammer into shape his shovel I realized I was seeing him make his first serious attempt at something productive. There had not been much evidence of anything organized or faintly constructive in his life of late. His latest domestic upheaval along with the subsequent loss of his job and then his health had all been factors crowding in upon him. Each demanding in time and thought, his attention and response never permitted him to concentrate on the task in hand, always summoning their own personal court of enquiry, desiring to know in hard, cold, calculating fact where he had gone wrong and how much he had contributed to the whole sorry scheme of things. All this soul-searching only left him with a rather sullen and gloomy disposition. Suddenly, his work completed to his apparent satisfaction, he made his way over to the welding section. A few tacks of welding would add the final touch to the finished article. Standing as I was alongside the welding bench with Brian, who was helping me to add the last remaining nine spots of solder to my doll's house, it was clear to me that Will's satisfaction with the finished article had also deep feelings of pride attached to it. Just a common or garden shovel, but perhaps it represented to him tangible evidence of his newfound ability to concentrate long enough to see a thing through to its successful conclusion. Dave, who was responsible for the welding on this particular day, was also answerable for much of the mischievous behaviour directed towards Will. Joining the queue, Will waited patiently to have his shovel attended to. His turn came and went and still Dave gave not the slightest indication of even recognizing Will. It soon became manifest that he was being purposely ignored. Others soon became aware of what was happening and Will once again became the centre of their unwelcome attention, the object of their teasing. This was the final match which set the fuse alight. Something within Will exploded he headed straight for his bench picking up his hammer. Then, shovel in one hand, hammer in the other, he made for the anvil with grim determination. He laid his shovel upon the anvil almost like Abraham in the act of offering up his greatest gift. Only no divine intervention stayed Will's hand. In a frenzy, his hammer rained down blow after blow upon his shovel, beating it into a clump of twisted metal. But this gesture, dramatic as it was, could not contain the full magnitude of his intense feeling of frustration and hostility. The next obvious outlet for his aggression was Dave the welder who was standing a few feet away from us. Giving a wild cry of rage, Will raised the hammer above his head and flung it with hysterical force towards the instigator of his fury, mercifully missing Dave but passing between Brian and me in its flight before striking the wall with an impact which, to say the least, was shattering. Then, rebounding off the wall, its speed considerably weakened by its encounter with the wall's resistance but none the less still at a force to be reckoned with, the hammer struck Brian and opened up quite a cut on his forehead. Meanwhile, Will stood like Cú Chulainn defending Ulster by facing his enemies, the men of Ireland. Blocking all means of escape, he challenged one and all to engage with him in mortal combat. Back among the welding equipment, the helpless Brian tried in vain to pick himself up from the floor. 'Come on who'll be next?' screamed Will, the gleam of triumph in his eyes and the smell of victory in his nostrils. Needless to say there were no takers. By now Will was literally foaming at the mouth and gesticulating in an unmistakable fashion as he continued to hurl out challenge after challenge. After a while it became noticeable that a considerable gap had occurred between Will and his antagonists. The bottom of our workshop had unexpectedly gained a popularity hitherto unknown. But Will was not finished yet. More was to follow. Having sensed he was the man of the moment, the fellow in the big picture as it were, Will decided to press home his advantage. It was they who waited with bated breath on his every movement and he was not going to disappoint them. With a mad roar he made his charge, at the same time looking around frantically for another weapon. What followed closely resembled one of these old sped-up films of the Keystone Cops as every available window became a means of escape. Even the most seriously handicapped among us found undreamed of sources of energy to call on in their mad scramble to escape the wrath of this once docile giant. In a matter of seconds the building was empty and big Will reigned supreme, a solitary figure in his moment of triumph. The final summing up to all this was left to the superintendent in charge of training, who obviously was in receipt of information regarding Will's medical history. He left us in no doubt that the consequences for interfering with Will in any way, or any recurrence of any such similar incidents, would end in the termination of the contract of employment of those involved.

Chapter 18
R.D.P. and All That

With my two months at the training scheme completed I joined the ranks of the unemployed, soon to discover the disadvantages for one so young in holding a blue card. Many firms exploited the R.D.P. (Regional Development Programme) by offering a light job with wages to match, expecting one, as a disabled person, to be receiving some form of pension that would supplement the low wages offered. As a young man of twenty I was in receipt of no such pension and was therefore unsuitable for most positions offered to the holder of a blue card. As I would have been working for wages less than half the average, with quite a number of such experiences behind me, I decided to take steps to rectify the situation by discarding my blue card and taking my chances without one, signing on for normal employment with no strings attached, no favours asked, prepared to meet any commitment.

The Belfast City Council (or some other responsible body) decided that the electric cables in the Belfast area required changing from DC to AC. The wisdom of my decision to relinquish my blue card was put to the most stringent test for, in consequence of the proposed alterations to the electric cables, the Electricity Highway Department increased their outdoor staff by another forty men conscripted from the Bureau on a temporary basis until the changeover was complete. As a result of all this, completely ignorant of what was expected of me, I reported to the main power station at Albert Bridge attired, as part of my working clothes, in blue jeans and a pair of slip-ons. We arrived on the site in the Glengormley area on the back of an open lorry. Our first task was helping the squad to pull the high tension cable along a cut in the road. It was well into winter and the trench, known as the cut, in which we were expected to work, was filled with mud formed by the rain. I remember standing looking into the cut and then looking apprehensively at my unsuitable footwear till a voice yelled out, 'Come on, don't be afraid of it, get in among it.' Taking a deep breath I ruefully jumped into the cut, grabbing hold of the cable and pulling in response to the shrill whistle from the ganger, finding as I did so that on each alternative heave of the cable, which took me further down the cut, I had to retrace my steps in order to retrieve my slip-ons that were left behind, stuck fast in the mud. My first day, as can be imagined, was a total disaster from the start. My feet were in a mess and my hands were raw flesh. Long before the finishing time of 5.30 p.m. I was already beginning to yearn for the more sheltered existence promised to the R.D.P. But that was all behind me now and I was more than ever determined to take my chance without a blue card. However, with winter fast upon us, there were moments when I must confess I doubted the sanity of my decision and the wisdom of tempting the Almighty on such a vital issue as my health, particularly on those occasions when we had to shovel the snow off the flagstones before we could even dig them up.

Crossing the street is an almost unconscious exercise, as conventional and matter of fact as putting out the cat with the milk bottles or halting at the kerb until the traffic passes, but to cross the street with the aid of a drift and a seven-pound hammer is quite another experience altogether and one guaranteed to leave a deep and lasting impression on those so involved. I can well remember how, as a team of four, we encircled the drift, a sort of giant chisel. Each equipped with a seven-pound hammer, we set to work, each one following the other, rather awkwardly at first until we had entered into the rhythm or the swing, as blow after blow sank the drift deeper and deeper into the concrete. It was after such bouts of strenuous activity that I was subject to fits of depression as I wondered whether my collapsed lung could stand up to the physical demands being made on it. To counteract this I adopted a form of self-hypnosis or, as

I believe it's called, auto-suggestion, repeating to myself day after day that things would get better. Hard work seemed to be agreeing with me. But soon, despite the suggestions of the ganger of my squad to the contrary, after six months and the changeover completed, in common with the other temporary men, I was put on my notice. It was to be quite some time before I was to find constant employment, almost two years in fact, during which time I had the soul-destroying experience of signing on at the Labour Exchange (the Bureau) in Corporation Street.

Twice a week we made our pilgrimage down to this 'Temple of Gloom'. As its devotees we rededicated ourselves in preparation for our next weekly visit by presenting ourselves at its confessional box. Here we reaffirmed our identity with the thousands of adherents by the simple but damming confession, made during the act of signing, for which, as a single man, I received the princely sum of two pounds. It was here I was constantly meeting a cross section of my old friends from both sides of the religious divide, the friendships created over a period stretching now to three years since my illness. Most of them had given up all hope of ever finding employment. This for me was the most depressing aspect of my visits to this Temple of Gloom. In a country where men were chasing jobs instead of vice versa, there was obviously intense competition in the field of employment. Therefore the odds on for an unemployed person with no qualifications and an adverse medical history getting a job were very remote indeed. In those days, strange as it may seem, the obstacles to obtaining suitable employment were immense. One could have fallen at any number of hurdles including where preference was given to those who had previous experience. This was very off-putting to say the least, especially when it applied to the most menial of jobs for which the qualifications required could have been met by a half intelligent chimpanzee. Then, of course, there were those areas of employment whose doors were opened only to the ex-service, as in the Post Office, apart from those lucky enough to start as Telegram boys.

If I had felt some stigma attached to my illness it was mild in comparison to that which I felt as a member of the unemployed. In our country their name was legion because they were many and their unhappy predicament no less evil. For some reason, rightly or wrongly, I always felt that my illness was inevitable, something over which I had no control and had to accept, while being unemployed was to be involved in a number of complex and far-reaching issues, some of which I have already mentioned, some bound up with economics, others implying causes that were more personal in origin. My own feelings on this issue were torn between a sense of personal failure and resentment against a country geared to such an acceptable level of unemployment, where such a large percentage of the population is denied the basic essentials of life, the right to work and plan for the future, where unemployment was fast being regarded as a necessary social evil. Here were men who barely eked out an existence, identified by their worn and shiny clothes. The drawn, staring faces were immediately recognizable, depicting lives barren and empty, while other men were occupied with simple domestic demands like facing the problem of whether they could afford another babysitter this week, or if it would be Blackpool or Butlins this year, or wise to speculate their savings on a new car. The temple devotee's demands are much more simple in content but more demanding and inward-looking. The problem changing from whether he can afford a babysitter to whether he can afford a baby. The car becomes the need for a pram. Holidays to Blackpool and Butlins give place to the enforced holiday which fate has organized for him at Fender Park (This was a humorous term used to mean beside the fireplace). We speak of their problems to make ends meet, but the ends are not the real issue; life's problems have always a beginning and an end however inglorious. To the unemployed man, always by necessity more practically-minded in his approach to life, it's not the ends but the in-between that demands their attention: the grocery bill still outstanding at the wee shop around the corner, the tired look on his wife's face and the sudden realization that the real world outside is passing them by. I had seen it all many times written in the faces of the men who had become my friends. It was little wonder that some of my fellow unemployed, if I may use the term, resorted to bitterness and hostile criticism of their lot. A constant topic among us, and one which I resented, was the unequal distribution of wealth and the way society was organized from the top to keep the underdog down. To me, a devout loyalist, it all seemed suspiciously close to treason. Yet in our own working-class area of Sandy Row, during all the flag-waving and ballyhoo of election, we were asked to vote for men or women who were either out of touch or completely indifferent to our own existing social conditions. In those days, like those of my father, we put no price tag on our election loyalty. My father would often say when we voiced any criticism of the local candidate, 'It's the party that counts not the man.' I guess we sold our election loyalty cheaply in those days.

As I left our street on my twice-weekly visits to the Bureau I was always deeply conscious, rightly or wrongly, that there were those few individuals in our district who watched my departure with a great deal of interest and comment. It was as if I could hear them reiterate the fantasies of my own mind, 'There he goes again, I doubt if he ever intends to work again, he is not a patch on his father.' But imagination gave way to reality when these same individuals, who in my flights of fantasy appeared to challenge my lack of initiative in seeking work, confronted me in the real world with such remarks as 'You have a great time of it', and 'Your life's a holiday.' Little did they know that inwardly I hated those remarks, which I found so hurtful, and I never left our street for those early morning trips to the Bureau, without feeling pursued by a hundred eyes all passing judgment on me, measuring me against the stature of my father who had never missed a day at work in his life.

During those summer evenings when the activity of the church had ceased, I would take myself out as soon as we had our evening meal, not returning again until dusk. This ritual which I indulged in was performed not from any feelings of self-pity, but rather from a sincere feeling that I should not be present when my father, after his long twelve-hour working day, sought the comfort and relaxation of our home. To me it would have been almost profane to have been around and to be thought of as sharing it with him. It was the only time in my life, during the periods of unemployment, that I felt I had nothing in common with him. How I hated these strange feelings that threatened to take possession of me. How I hated the whole dreadful business, hated the bitterness and the hate that was building up inside me, hated a maturity twice my years' of experience, but a gleam of hope arose on the horizon. It was in the autumn of 1960 and the weekly refills maintaining the partial collapse of my lung were terminated, now all of three years since the first initial collapse of my lung. Fortune smiled on me following this and I obtained a job.

Before continuing Gordon's story, there is another chapter which we believe he wrote, but it is missing. It dealt with his experiences in a number of jobs. His daughter Julie provided the following information:

'My father worked in a number of jobs, including a jam factory and other jobs. Most of his time would have been working for the Belfast City Council as a bin man. It was about 1966 that he happily started work in the Ulster Museum as a Gallery Attendant, but soon became a supervisor and due to his undoubted ability, he was promoted to the post of Chief Warder. He also served as a part-time member of the Ulster Defence Regiment. While working in the museum, daddy's passion was to continue educating himself by getting O levels and A levels in Maths, English and Irish history. That led to him going on to graduate in Irish social history and obtain a BA and Master's degree in 1983, the year before daddy sadly passed away on 5th November 1984. So glad he made it, we are so very proud of him.'

Julie Leckie

Chapter 19
The Reaching Out

There is another more personal and spiritual part of my life responsible, to a large extent, for my outlook and attitudes to life, just as much a part of me as my sight, sound, hearing, smell and touch. A part of me which I have in my previous reflections quite purposely only alluded to. I have felt it necessary to follow the awareness and development of this spiritual aspect of my experiences in Sandy Row, which I see inherent in man as an unconscious reaching out to something or someone beyond man himself. Therefore, I would like to follow my own spiritual awareness in my own experience and the influence of those institutions which cater for and influence this deep craving within man. Whether we regard this reaching out as acquired and developed by a process of evolution arising out of the earliest attitudes of our ancestors, or whether we believe this spiritual faculty, this reaching out, is an inseparable part of our make-up, whatever we believe, few, I think, will deny the existence of this almost reflex action which we call reaching out, and which has been responsible for those experiences, particularly under tremendous emotional stress and strain, we are apt to call religious. My earliest contact with those institutions geared to meet this human need in man was as a babe at my mother's side. This was refreshed in my mind as I came across an old picture presented to my mother on which was inscribed the following text, 'God commended his love towards us in that while we were yet sinners Christ died for us.' The reverse side declared that it had been presented to her for attendance at the Belfast City Mission Hall Bible Class for Women. This class took place in the Mission Hall, situated on the railway bridge almost opposite Utility Street. The missionary's name, I think, was Mr Hey. I can vaguely remember those weekday classes as a child, some impressions more vivid and lasting than others. Just as if it was only yesterday, I can still see the wooden forms, the women adorned with some form of bonnet or other (my mother usually wore a beret), the appropriated scripture text – 'Ye Must Be Born Again' – in scroll form painted on the wall immediately behind the platform clearly visible for all the congregation to see and contemplate. Then there was the rustling sound of paper occasionally violating the silence, in competition with the continual drone of the gas heater, as a hand dipped into a pocket to select a boiled sweet, discreetly slipped into the mouth under the pretence of using a handkerchief while the missionary, equipped with blackboard and visual aids, and with great enthusiasm and inspiration, led his little congregation through the journeys of the children of Israel, from their enforced captivity and hurried departure from Egypt until their arrival in the promised land. And always there was the smell peculiar to the red-backed and well-worn Redemption Hymn Books, whose hymns were a particular favourite of mine with their rousing tunes and choruses. Not necessarily my own favourite, but the hymn which I always associated with those little Bible classes was, 'When he cometh to make up his jewels'. Somehow or other, out of these classes, as probably the only male present, I can remember some sort of exhortation to forgo the evils of make-up and the reference to lips rather unattractively identified with painted cart wheels, no doubt a reference to the red painted spokes and rims of the wooden wheels of the various horse-drawn carts. The small hall was usually packed, for those were the days following the outbreak of war when religion was a popular spiritual exercise. And we were no doubt prayerfully hopeful that God would lead us out of this terrible war situation as he did Moses from the land of Egypt, for this was the era of the cottage meeting and it was amazing the homes, which underwent a sudden change of attitudes in the threat of this global confrontation, that opened their doors for prayer and religious meetings. The early church similarly availed itself of this means of grace but for obviously different reasons.

St Paul at one time made reference to the church in your house. In our home at No. 12 we had a large cupboard in a recess of the kitchen beginning halfway up the wall that was literally crammed full of books all belonging to my father and which could only be reached by standing on a chair. Every time the cupboard was opened, the books came tumbling out all over the place. It was on occasions like this that I was usually around to pick up a certain book that was particularly interesting to me, although I was as yet unable to read the written word. Almost every other page, it seemed, contained an illustration connected with the coming of Christ, from a picture of Nebuchadnezzar's dream image as interpreted by Daniel, to a picture of Gabriel descending from the heavens complete with trumpet and scroll in which was written a decree concerning the latter days. I have a feeling now that this book or books of a similar nature found their way into most homes in and around Sandy Row.

None of this zeal for religion had obviously any meaning for my young life, even my first real participation in religious instruction as I started school failed to achieve any meaningful response from me. During those dark winter mornings in Workman School we usually began our day by singing some appropriate stanza like,

Jesus bids us shine
With a pure, clear light,
Like a little candle Burning in the night.
In this world of darkness
So let us shine
You in your small corner,
And I in mine.

As I sung this hymn, my thoughts ran at variance with the true spiritual application of the hymn. For me the world of darkness mentioned by the hymn writer was a real physical reality that I accepted as part of our winter set-up but personally dreaded. The analogy of a candle burning in the night was hardly designed to fill my youthfulness with any real enthusiasm either, as the night and dark mornings were parts of my life which I usually identified with the end of play and time for bed, and the morning after dark with the dark forebodings of what lay ahead for me personally in the school curriculum. Added to this, any spiritual meaning the hymn, or indeed any hymn, may have had was lost to me due to the all-pervading and frightening personality of Miss Tate, which for me pervaded the atmosphere like some sinister influence dominating and dampening any form of self-expression on my part. I was simply terrified of the woman.

My evacuation to the country brought me, as a young child, in contact with the family side of prayer, as practised by my three cousins. All slightly older than myself, they had come to stay with us for a short while and were given to praying as a family unit. This was something which I was invited to identify myself with. They were simple prayers asking God to bless and protect our respective families and bring about a speedy end to the war. In our country school, I was always confused when we opened in prayer as to why little Pat, who sat next to me, vacated the room until our exhortations were concluded. It was only years later that I realized, she must have been of a different religion to me. It was not until I had to leave Workman School, which I had restarted after my return from the country, that I felt any conscious need to use this spiritual faculty. There were moments in my early days at my new school at Fane Street when I found myself consciously expressing the following prayer in the words of the well-known hymn, 'I need Thee every hour, stay Thou nearby.'

This is my first remembrance of a conscious need to reach out and one which I realize now was born out of necessity. So religious experience began for me on the simple basis of need, similar to that which prompted people during the war to reach out, motivated by a feeling of helplessness and necessity. At this stage of my life I was eleven and dealing with the miniature crises in my life that came with the start of a new school. That period passed and now I no longer felt any need to reach outward, but viewed life once more with the healthy anticipation of a growing eleven-year-old. I was over seventeen before I once more felt this need to reach out. This sprang from a crisis in my life involving a loss of health, which I was totally unaware of at the time, and some deep feelings of teenage guilt. This reaching out ended with an encounter and a commitment; in the terminology of our evangelical and Protestant theology, I was saved. This is a term which I was never happy with and never used with connotations that implied a dogmatic attitude to the furniture of heaven and the temperature of Hell. I had made a commitment of my life and as a result, I hope, a personal encounter. Certainly the whole course of my life was to change and my outlook was to undergo what I can only describe as a dynamic change. I had sought a word from the beyond for my human predicament and I had found it in that person of Jesus Christ, who pervades the pages of the New Testament and whose absence in our world, irrespective of what beliefs we hold concerning Him, would leave life for many of us like Hamlet without the Prince of Denmark, a tale told by an idiot full of sound and fury signifying nothing.

I became a member of that church whose tradition was born out of the spiritual experience of an Anglian clergyman by the name of John Wesley, who, in a little mission hall in Aldersgale Street, felt his heart strangely warmed. The Methodist church in return offered me a warm and rich experience of life for which I will always be grateful. As a result of my own spiritual experience I became an active member of Primitive Street Methodist Church, Sandy Row.

In those days Sandy Row was under the influence of what I would describe, without being over pious, as a real spiritual awakening. Open air meetings were commonplace and if it could be said there was a pub at almost every street corner, I think it would be fair to say that on a Saturday, in particular, each street corner was at some time or other visited by those people who were convinced that if the people did not go to church, the church must go to the people. Public houses were visited on a Saturday night by members of our church who distributed religious tracts on which were printed an invitation to attend the non-denominational men's meeting held in our church on a Sunday afternoon. This meeting reached a cross section of our Sandy Row community and provided a means of worship for many with very nominal church connections, who would not otherwise have been so exercised to attend a conventional church service.

Primitive Street Church itself was a flourishing church with a rich spiritual experience. This was due to a large extent to the efforts of one man, William Johnston. He was an old soldier of the 1914–18 war, a postman by profession with a deep religious experience going back many years. I can still see him as he stood at our Saturday night prayer meeting, his ink-stained fingers flicking over the pages of his pocket Testament, stopping only now and then to push his glasses back onto the bridge of his nose, his grey hair plentiful at the sides and bald on top. For me, his most dominating features were his eyes; they spoke volumes about the man. They were sad as the occasion demanded it, such as when he thought of lives wasted and homes broken, and twinkled with an inner peace and tranquillity as he commended his Saviour to the district. For William Johnston, Sandy Row and district was the burden God had laid on his heart. How often he would quote, 'Other vineyards have I kept but my own vineyard have I not kept.'[16] Here was a man with a vision, a man who regarded Sandy Row as a fertile mission field right on his very doorstep. It was in this mission field that he worked tirelessly with a determination and dedication which was inspiring and utterly unselfish. He was a totally committed Christian, absolutely loyal to the task in hand and for which, as he so often said, he was 'a fool for Christ'. He had equipped himself with a skin like a rhinoceros. He had a personal approach system in operation at the men's meeting, which I remember was literally packed every Sunday afternoon, due mainly to his follow-up policy of visitation. Every man was given, by Mr Johnston, a Gospel of St. John with a number on it. Thereafter, as he attended each Sunday, on entry he lifted a ring from a box at the door and placed it on his appropriate hook, which had a number corresponding to that on his Gospel of St. John. The numbers on the board had a range almost topping the three-hundred mark. Without fail this board was checked. A hook with a ring missing on it was sure to be

---

[16] Song of Solomon 1:6.

noticed and a visit prescribed. As he would so often say, on explaining the system at the meeting, 'the visitor is given a booklet of the Gospel of St. John with a number on it and from then on he is hooked.' I remember the incident related by one of those hooked on William Johnston's line, how as an absentee he had the prescribed visit. Seeing William Johnston pass his window, he ducked under the table in his little kitchen house when Mr Johnston, realizing what was up, opened the door and grabbed the foot protruding under the table shouting out as he did so, 'Come on out brother you're spied.'

His sense of loyalty to the men's meetings knew no bounds. When he should have been relaxing and enjoying the brisk sea air at Donaghadee on his yearly holiday, Sunday found him, as usual, engaged in his weekly task of supervising the issue of new booklets and the noting of unattended hooks. For him the struggle for the soul of Sandy Row and district was a constant one and if he needed any justification for this it was in his oft-repeated observations that 'The devil never takes a holiday.'

A great characteristic of the man was his tremendous respect and feeling for the dignity of man. More than once, as we prepared for our yearly day trip to the sea sponsored on behalf of the men of the meeting, he cautioned us all who attended the meetings to attach little importance to table etiquette. We had a tremendous lunch laid on for us, usually in Portrush, and for some in our meeting, whose only home comforts were those located in the Model lodging house in Matilda Street, this was quite an event in their lives. With this in mind he would implore us to pay little if any attention to the somewhat predictable table antics of a few of our members, and to act perfectly natural was the order of the day. After all, I suppose when one is faced with an appetizing plate of soup a spoon will not always suffice to remove the last vestige of that precious liquid food from a horizontally positioned plate, and what better way to obtain the desired results than to raise it to the mouth with the corresponding noises. We were instructed to completely ignore how some men behaved at the table. With regards the main meal he would remind us, with a twinkle in his eye, that any unconventional eating habits we might observe must be seen in the context of that well-established fact that there were fingers and thumbs before knives and forks.

What I would call my most vivid and characteristic picture of the man, and one which quite often springs to mind, is one which I never witnessed but never the less can relate as factual. It belonged to an era which I knew not of, when Primitive Street Methodist was in the middle of a spiritual crisis. The Saturday night meeting, always so well attended and from which a tremendous work both spiritual and social was accomplished, had fallen on hard times. In fact, for many weeks, indeed months, and perhaps who knows even longer, not a solitary figure entered the church at the appropriate time. He opened the meeting in prayer. His intersessions completed, he took up position behind the small organ and a rousing hymn was played and sung, and then a hallowed hush pervaded the little room as he took up the central position for the Bible reading. Not even a cough or a tread of a foot on a loose floorboard or a shuffle on a seat disturbed the sacred silence to reward him as his voice, calm and steady, projected itself around the empty. For stewards are called not so much to be successful but faithful, and what might seem to many to be a pointless exercise was providing a witness of one man's burden for a district that was constantly in his prayers, as no passer-by could fail to hear the strains of organ music played at a tempo which, whatever the hymn, sounded suspiciously like the tramping feet of 'Onward Christian Soldiers', or, more important still, notice the light from the window. This was one of the many sides to life in Sandy Row which I came to know and identify myself with, and although my personal beliefs and attitudes have changed with the years, I know at heart that the person which I now am, with my own personal views on life and standards of morality, belong not so much to me as an individual but to the culture and background of the district in which I was born and reared and for which I make no apology. A district which gave the figure of Christ, which from my earliest memories hung in our bedroom depicting a rather genial and benevolent figure embracing the children of the nations of the world, meaning and power through the lives of my many friends from the Row. Our only failing at times have been the emphasis put on the wrong questions we have asked each other about what we believe, when it should have been whom. One divides us, the other unites us.

> He drew a circle that shut me out
> Heretic rebel, a thing to flout.
> But Love and I had the wit to win:
> We drew a circle that took him in!

> – Edwin Markham

Gordon died on 5th November 1984, a true son of Sandy Row

The following poem which was written before the church was demolished was not mentioned by Gordon and he probably never knew about it. I am sure Gordon would have liked it and added it to his memories.

PRIMITIVE STREET METHODIST CHURCH
Plain bare seats of varnished pine
No comfort for the Wesleyan spine.
The Patterned ceiling, lifted high
To lift our thoughts beyond the sky.
Naked boards beneath the seat
For saints to rest their weary feet.
The modest organ, unadorned

That swelled in praise each Sabbath morn.
The choir seats; tiered against the wall
To sing of cross and babe and stall;
Of harvests ripening in the sun
And Easter when new life begun.
The half-moon pulpit, iron and wood
Where earnest preachers read and stood.
The chairs and table, loves last gift
Bore bread and wine, the heart to sift.
The communion of His blood they share
In memory of the sin he bore.
The heavy bible, black and bound
Where verses from his word were found.
The stained-glass windows, rainbowed light
Bore flowers and fruit and lilies white.
The twin blue aisles with aged creak
With patience bore the weighty meek.
To stand and sing, to sit and pray
For love and faith along life's way.
The two stout doors of Gothic make
Would welcome all for Jesus' sake;
And over all on painted wall
Like trumpet sound, or clarion call
The warning; that what ere you gain
You must, you must be born again.
And yet to me, how far more fair
Than wood or glass beyond compare

Are dearest friends, beloved and wise.
More friendlier, far in Paradise
Until by the Saviour's love to meet again in Heaven
Above…
For wood and glass and stone and lime are only sub-
stance made for time.

– Adam McKinley

Primitive Street Methodist Church

And finally, as the book started with the family home at 12
Gaffikin Street, so it should end with the historic street.
Gordon's mother and father continued to live at 12 Gaffikin
Street and remained there until, the 1980s, when the street

was demolished under a redevelopment scheme. This was the end for the little community that lived there.

An account of the last three years as a residential street was given by the then *Belfast Telegraph* reporter, Sandra Chapman who interviewed the remaining residents. It was a two-part series, Where Have All the People Gone? The report was published in the *Belfast Telegraph* on 17 and 18 August 1982 and is an excellent account of the street's final few years. It must have taken Sandra a considerable number of days to interview all the residents including Gordon's mother at number 12, who was by then, a widow. For those who would like to see Sandra's report, it can be seen on microfilm at the Newspaper Library, Belfast Central Library, Royal Avenue or online at The British Newspaper Archive.

Article from *Belfast Telegraph*

Princess Elizabeth and the Duke of Edinburgh visit to Sandy Row, 1949. The Boyne Bridge in the background being used as a viewing platform.

Oh, Sandy Row! oh, Sandy Row!
My heart is there, where'er I go;
The rivers they shall cease to flow,
Ere I forget thee, Sandy Row,
And Sandy Row, purse, heart, and hand,
Will stand for Queen and Fatherland.
The Bible and the Church we know,
Will guarded be in Sandy Row!

Gordon Freeman and his wife, Jane

Printed by Amazon Italia Logistica S.r.l.
Torrazza Piemonte (TO), Italy

56376105R00129